HEROES
BENEATH THE
WAVES

HEROES
BENEATH THE
WAVES

True Submarine Stories of the
Twentieth Century

MARY NIDA SMITH

Skyhorse Publishing
A Herman Graf Book

Skyhorse Publishing books may be purchased in bulk at special discounts for sales promotion, corporate gifts, fund-raising, or educational purposes. Special editions can also be created to specifications. For details, contact the Special Sales Department, Skyhorse Publishing, 307 West 36th Street, 11th Floor, New York, NY 10018 or info@skyhorsepublishing.com.

Skyhorse® and Skyhorse Publishing® are registered trademarks of Skyhorse Publishing, Inc.®, a Delaware corporation.

Visit our website at www.skyhorsepublishing.com.

10 9 8 7 6 5 4 3 2 1

Library of Congress Cataloging-in-Publication Data is available on file.

Cover design by Qualcom

Print ISBN: 978-1-63450-512-3
Ebook ISBN: 978-1-5107-0046-8

Printed in the United States of America

Dedication

I dedicate this book to my husband, Melvin T. Smith, who served sixteen years in submarines, and to all the submarine veterans who lived and died providing freedom to many countries. I am grateful to the men who shared their stories in my book so that school-children, submarine veterans' families, and others would have a greater understanding of what these men endured.

Acknowledgments

God is first in my life, and He has directed me throughout this book.

Thank you to Cynthia Esty for taking me to the Ozark Writers League meeting in May 2014, where I first met my literary agent, Jeanie Loiacono. When I found out that Jeanie had an opening on her pitch list, I approached her, and she greeted me with open arms. She said she'd love to represent my first book, *Submarine Stories of World War II*. She soon found that Skyhorse Publishing was interested in extending the stories to cover all the wars since—and thus was born this book, *War Beneath the Waves*.

Alathea Daniels is knowledgeable regarding electronic format and submission—which I was not. She has helped me in the editing process as well as getting this book into the form required.

I want to especially thank the following people for allowing me to use their photos: Mark R. Clary, Robert L. DeVore Sr., Joel Greenberg, Loyal A. Huson, Hank Kudzik, Cliff Kuykendall, Michael K. Mohl, Larry Ofner, Norman "Red" Stein, Melvin T. Smith, and Robert D. Wilcox. Special credit goes to Jeff Kelly for his photo of the *Guardfish* (SSN-612) and the *Daniel Webster* (SSBN-626).

A special thank you to the following veterans: George Arnold, president of the USS *Sea Fox* SS402 Association; Joel Greenberg,

Commander USSVI, Tucson, Arizona Base, and editor of "The Open Hatch" and "Below Decks Log" newsletters; and Robert L. DeVore, editor, *Polaris,* the official publication of U.S. Submarine Veterans of World War II.

Thank you to Kevin Copeland, Commander, Submarine Force Atlantic Public Affairs, and Wanda Kudzik Frecks (daughter of Hank Kudzik).

Some of the stories in this book were published in submarine magazines such as *Polaris*, the official publication of U.S. Submarine Veterans of World War II, the longest running magazine dedicated to submariners [pronounced sub-marine-ers] of that era. Another publication, *American Submariner* (published by United States Submarine Veterans Inc.) was formed for men who served after World War II. This group is dedicated to all who have served and still are serving on submarines, protecting our freedoms. Many of the World War II submarine veterans joined this group as their local or state chapters were decommissioned.

Many of these stories written by the submarine veterans were submitted to me. Some are reprinted exactly, and some I have written from compiled information. I am thankful to each of these men. I also thank my husband, Melvin Tolbert Smith, for checking facts and terminology. Between the covers of this book are battle stories that bring to light the sacrifices made in WWII, and also honor those who have carried out their duties since that time. I am deeply grateful to all veterans who have served and are still serving.

I am dedicated to sharing stories of these men who have kept their stories within them for so long. The government may never release all their records, which continue to be kept secret by these men who served in what is known as the "Silent Service." Wives, children, grandchildren, and families deserve to understand the personalities of these men and how their experiences affected and continue to affect them.

I am proud to be a sub-vet wife and to have had the privilege of writing and compiling these stories. My hope is that this book will be read not only by military veterans, but by veterans' children, grandchildren, and great-grandchildren, and that they will comment, "Gosh! My dad (granddad, uncle, brother, friend) did that? He was a hero!"

—Mary Nida Smith

Table of Contents

Preface

The first submarine used for combat by the United States was the *Turtle*, a hand-propelled, egg-shaped submersible built for service during the American Revolution. A submarine was also built for service during the Civil War, and many were placed in service at the beginning of the twentieth century, during World War I. Many of these World War I submarines were still in service at the beginning of World War II, but two hundred submarines were built specifically for use in World War II. In the summer of 1944, American shipyards delivered submarines at the rate of six per month.

The standard inside measurements of submarines during World War II were 265 feet in length and twenty-four feet in width. The submarine force consisted of 50,000 men, with 16,000 of them serving inside of the submarines. During the four years after the Japanese attack on Pearl Harbor, fifty-two U.S. submarines were sent to the bottom of the sea. It was on the operating submarines that roughly 18 percent of submariners gave their lives for their country.

Between December 7, 1941, and August 14, 1945, a submarine personnel force of less than 2 percent of the total U.S. Naval combat strength inflicted a staggering 55 percent of Japan's maritime losses—but the victory was costly. They had the highest combat casualty rate of any portion of America's World War II military.

U.S. submarine prisoners of war (POWs) in World War II comprise a long list of names—some have returned and some have not. These are listed at http://www.subvetpaul.com/POWs. htm, a page that was last updated in 2005. The memory of those U.S. submarines lost in World War II and their men, who are still on "Eternal Patrol," will never be forgotten. They are honored at every Submarine Veterans of World War II and USSVI meeting and conference by the ringing of the bells. Fifty-two out of 288 boats were lost, along with more than 374 officers and 3,131 enlisted men. The U.S. submarines took out 1,178 enemy ships (cargo, tanker, and transport)—plus 214 naval vessels.

The heroes who fought the battles below the oceans and four seas have for the most part worked unnoticed. Patiently watching and listening, these heroes never cried out, "Look at us. We helped win the war!" From the American Revolution to the Civil War; to World War I, World War II, Korea, Vietnam, and the Cold War; to today's more modern concerns, U.S. submarines have patrolled and fought for our freedoms. The Submarine Force celebrated their 100th centennial on October 5, 1999. They continue to be the "silent heroes," building their memorials to be part of history and hoping that someday the reminders would cause people to war no more.

Life Under the Water:
Statistics & Interesting Submarine Facts

THE FIRST SUBMERSIBLES

The history of "submersibles"—airtight, rigid diving vehicles, either remote or manned, designed for exploration while completely submerged in water—is fairly recent, but many are surprised to hear that such inventions have been traced back over 500 years. The earliest known example of such a vehicle is shown in a painting from 1500s India that shows Alexander the Great being lowered in a glass diving bell.

Around 1620, Dutch engineer Cornelis Drebbel built submersibles that resembled two wooden rowboats—one atop the other—made from grease-soaked leather stretched on a frame with oars stuck through waterproofed holes.

When designed for warfare, these submersibles are called "submarines," and the men who man them are called "submariners" (pronounced sub-marine-ers). What were the early submariners like, and what would it feel like to know you are going into combat for the first time in an environment where if your ship is destroyed you remain under the water? How can you store enough air in the compartments for all those men? What and how did they eat? The following facts and statistics will answer some of these questions, but in this book you'll also meet many of the men who experienced life on a submarine, and you'll hear their stories in their own words.

* * *

In 1776, Yale student David Bushnell built a hand-propelled, egg-shaped, two-propeller (for forward/backward and ascending/descending motion) submarine for the Americans during the American Revolution. This first combatant submarine was called the *Turtle*, and it carried explosive powder into battle. Some refer to this as the first use of a "torpedo." Bushnell was the only person capable of competently using this one-man submarine's combat functions, but due to physical impairments, he was not able to man the sub in any of its combat missions against British ships. Even so, General George Washington gave Bushnell a commission as an Army engineer, and later he became commander of the U.S. Army Corps of Engineers stationed at West Point.

About twenty years later, while studying in Paris in 1797, American inventor Robert Fulton developed the submarine *Nautilus*, a cucumber-shaped vessel slightly over twenty-one feet that contained the first "conning" tower (a glass eye for steering). He used Bushnell's hand-turned propeller for power, but used compressed air to raise the vessel and as an oxygen supply, with rudders for vertical and horizontal control. This submarine was tested by Napoleon. Fulton eventually built an armored submarine for the United States that carried ninety men. Robert Fulton has also been credited as the inventor of the steamboat.

Horace Hunley designed the CSS *H.L. Hunley*, a submarine launched in 1863 and used by the Confederacy in the blockade of Charleston. There is more about this submarine later in this book.

Jules Verne, in his great masterpiece *Twenty Thousand Leagues Under the Sea*, described in 1870 his vision of a great underwater vessel, the *Nautilus* (named the same as Robert Fulton's underwater invention of 1797), and its captain, Nemo, who considered it his mission to roam the globe supporting struggles against tyrannical oppression. Many of Verne's high technology and visionary ideas have since been created, and his work has merited a special article on the U.S. Navy website.

In 1893, at the request of the U.S. government, John Philip Holland built the USS *Plunger*, but he realized in the fall of 1896 that he had failed. He then built his sixth submarine, which was commissioned the USS *Holland* on October 12, 1900.

AVERAGE AGE OF SUBMARINERS

The average age of submariners during World War II was nineteen. The average age of submariners during the Cold War was twenty-three. As time has gone by, older submariners have been recalled to service, since they have had the necessary personality and experience to work in the close and exacting environment of a submarine. Every submariner must know his and everyone else's job. Normally, the crew takes turns at different posts. It makes sense to utilize the experience of veterans of the subs.

AVERAGE HEADCOUNT IN A TYPICAL SUBMARINE

Submarine crew size depends on the type and class of submarine, but a typical U.S. Navy submarine crew consists of fourteen officers, eighteen chief petty officers (senior enlisted men), and 109 other enlisted men.

HOW LONG CAN A SUBMARINE STAY SUBMERGED?

A diesel-electric submarine can stay at sea as long as its supply of fuel lasts, and as long as it is able to snorkel to recharge batteries. In the early days, oxygen was also a consideration. Today's nuclear submarines can stay submerged for more than ninety days, and are only limited by the food that is stored.

HOW DEEP CAN A SUBMARINE GO?

In the beginning, submarines would go approximately 300 feet deep. However, today's U.S. Navy submarines can submerge deeper than 800 feet. The actual depth is classified.

HOW MANY SUBS WERE IN SERVICE IN WWII?

It is hard to believe the number of submarines that were put into service during World War II that were made so early in the century. One can only imagine what might have gone through a new submariner's mind as he readied himself for his first mission aboard a submarine that had been built for World War I. The following is a list of the numbers of submarines of various classes that were used during World War II.

Submarine Class	No. of Submarines	Year Commissioned
O-Class Submarines	7	1918
R-Class Submarines	18	1918–1919
S-Class Submarines	38	1920–1922
B-Class Submarines	3	1925–1927
Argonaut Submarine	1	1928
Narwhal Submarines	2	1930
Dolphin-Class Submarine	1	1932
Cachalot-Class Submarines	2	1933–1934
Porpoise-Class Submarines	10	1935–1937
Salmon-Class Submarines	6	1937–1938
Sargo-Class Submarines	10	1939

Tambor-Class Submarines	6	1940–1941
Mackeral-Class Submarines	2	1941
Gar-Class Submarines	6	1941
Gato-Class Submarines	73	1941–1943
Balao-Class Submarines	115	1943–1945
Tench-Class Submarines	28	1944–1945

THE PERCENTAGE OF SUBS AND THEIR SINK RANKING

Less than 2 percent of U.S. sailors served in submarines, yet that small percentage sank over 30 percent of Japan's navy, including one battleship, eight aircraft carriers, and eleven cruisers. They also sank almost five million tons of shipping—over 60 percent of the Japanese merchant marine, causing great harm to the Japanese economy. In this effort, the Submarine Force lost fifty-two boats and 3,506 men.

During World War II, American submarines and their crew sank:

1   Battleship
4   Large aircraft carriers
4   Small aircraft carriers
3   Heavy cruisers
9   Light cruisers
43   Destroyers
23   Large submarines
1,113   Merchant ships of more than 500 tons

WHY WAS THE SINKING OF JAPANESE MERCHANT SHIPS DURING WORLD WAR II SO IMPORTANT?

The Japanese empire was an island empire, and if all those ships got through with all that food, fuel, tanks, trucks, troops, planes, guns, and ammunition, thousands and thousands more American sailors, soldiers, marines, and fliers would have been maimed or killed. In all, U.S. submarines sank more than 55 percent of all ships sunk—more than surface ships, Navy air, and the Air Corp. combined. They laid mines, hauled ammunition, transported troops, rescued refugees, deployed secret agents, delivered guerilla leaders, and rescued 504 fliers (including George H. W. Bush). They also had the highest loss rate of any Navy unit.

Please remember these facts the next time you see the U.S. Submarine emblem.

BITS AND PIECES

Submarines entered the navy fleet in 1900, where the first was named *Holland* in honor of John Holland, a submarine designer and builder. Later, submarines were given names such as *Grampus, Salmon,* and *Porpoise.* Some were given names of stinging creatures, such as the *Adder, Tarantula,* and *Viper.* Submarines were renamed in 1911 with alphanumeric names, such as A-i, C-i, 11-3, and L-7, until 1931. In 1931, they started naming them after fish and other residents of the sea.

While out to sea during War World II from 1939–1945, during lifeguard duty, submarine crews rescued over 520 downed airmen. They evacuated civilian refugees when needed. Patrol duration could be up to eighty-three days before any shore duty was assigned.

Diesel engine submarines were launched in 1912 and were used during World War I (1914–1918) and into World War II

(1939–1945). They didn't start numbering them until 1913, and during war patrols the numbers were removed. There were fifty-six boats in the U.S. Submarine Fleet that were assigned to the Pacific at the outbreak of war in December 1941.

At the beginning of WWII, lithe submarines were plagued with dud torpedoes. Some shot at an angle or not at all. The USS *Tang* shot one, and it came back like a boomerang and blew the boat that sent it. It took two years after the attack on Pearl Harbor before U.S. submarines had torpedoes that worked consistently.

The submarines and their crews performed many tasks, including evacuating the Philippine government, stopping enemy countries from receiving goods for their military and civilians, secret surveillance, and gathering weather data, photographing enemy shorelines through the periscopes, as well as carrying ammunition to the troops and rescuing civilians and nuns and other missionaries. In February 1942, the USS *Trout* arrived in Pearl Harbor with twenty-five million dollars of Philippines gold and silver.

Every crew member and officer was a volunteer—the cream of the fleet. It took a special person who could take orders. Everyone had to get along with their fellow crew members, for they would become a close family—a brotherhood. For many days while submerged, they saw no sunlight or stars, and they would not even smell the fresh salty air.

It could take six months to a year to put a newly constructed submarine into commission. One patrol run could make a sailor change his mind once he returned to shore. If he did, he was assigned to a "tin can"—a destroyer, anti-submarine escort vessel with about 150 to 200 crew members. Roughly one-third of the crew transferred or was disqualified after their first run.

Due to the urgent need for submarines during World War II, many of the crew went to sea without time to learn the basics. Crew members who at first thought they would be able to handle the confined quarters, the sounds, and the fear—serious realities in a submarine—but were unable to do the job that they were asked to do, were often sent to other areas of Navy service. At times, commanders were relieved of their command and accused of not being aggressive while on war patrols.

The Manitowoc Company shipbuilders in Manitowoc, Wisconsin, where some of the submarines were built, sailed with their assigned captains and crews to Chicago to be placed in dry dock barges. Later, the barges were transported down the Mississippi River to New Orleans. After the final fit-out in New Orleans, the submarines started their war patrols in the Pacific Theater.

Into the mid-1970s, attack submarines continued to be named for sea creatures. However, a few were named for legislators such as Richard B. Russell and L. Mendel Rivers.

When a submarine and its crew were overdue for their shore duty or new assignment, they were presumed "missing in action." Families at home received this message of their loved ones, but always held out that they would return, because many did.

Some torpedo men wrote their loved ones' names on the torpedoes. As each one fired, the man would say, "Go get them, honey!"

"Loose lips sink ships," as they did during World War II, when a congressman on the House Military Affairs Committee returned from a war zone visit and reported to the press that the Japanese depth charges were not deep enough, and that our submarines were out of harm's way. This cost the Americans ten submarines and 800 officers and men. From that time on, the submarine forces were known as "The Silent Service."

In 2000, the U.S. Postal Service issued a commemorative stamp series on submarines in honor of the 100th anniversary of submarine service.

"Eternal Patrol"
In Memory of the Fifty-two Submarines Lost in World War II
December 10, 1941–August 6, 1945

U.S. Navy submarines paid heavily for their success in World War II. A total of 374 officers and 3,131 men are on board these fifty-two U.S. submarines, "Still on Patrol."

"We shall never forget that it was our submarines that
held the lines against the enemy
while our fleets replaced losses and repaired wounds."
—Fleet Admiral C. W. Nimetz, USN

"I can assure you that they went down fighting and that
their brothers who survived them took a grim toll of our
savage enemy to avenge their deaths."
—Vice Admiral C. A. Lockwood Jr., USN, Commander
Submarine Force 1943–1945

December 10, 1941
Sealion (SS-195)
Four men lost
Sunk by aerial bombs

January 20, 1942
(S-36) (SS-141)
No loss of life
Ran aground

January 24, 1942
(S-26) (SS-131)
Forty-six men lost, two survivors
Rammed by escort

February 11, 1942
Shark I (SS-174)
Fifty-eight men lost
Sunk by surface craft

March 3, 1942
Perch (SS-176)
Eleven men lost. All taken prisoner
Eight died in prisoner of war camp
Sunk by surface craft

June 19, 1942
(S-27) (SS-132)
No loss of life
Ran aground

August 1, 1942
Grunion (SS-216)
Seventy men lost
Sunk cause unknown

August 16, 1942
(S-39) (SS-144)
No loss of life
Ran aground

January 10, 1943
Argonaut (SS-166)
One hundred and five men lost
Sunk by surface craft

February 16, 1943
Amberjack (SS-219)
Seven-four men lost
Sunk by surface craft and aerial bombs

March 5, 1943
Grampus (SS-207)
Seventy-one men lost
Sunk by surface craft

March 15, 1943
Triton (SS-201)
Seventy-four men lost
Sunk by surface craft

April 3, 1943
Pickerel (SS-177)
Seventy-four men lost
Sunk by surface craft

April 22, 1943
Grenadier (SS-210)
Four men lost, all taken prisoner
Four died in prisoner of war camp
Sunk by aerial bombs

May 28, 1943
Runner (SS-275)
Seventy-eight men lost
Sunk by enemy mines

June 12, 1943
(R-12) (SS-89)
Forty-two men lost, three survivors
Sunk cause unknown

August 29, 1943
Pompano (SS-181)
Seventy-six men lost
Sunk by enemy mines

September 12, 1943
Grayling (SS-209)
Seventy-six men lost
Sunk cause unknown

September 28, 1943
Cisco (SS-290)
Seventy-six men lost
Sunk by surface craft and aerial bombs

October 7, 1943
(S-44) (SS-155)
Fifty-five men lost, two survivors taken prisoner
Sunk by surface craft

October 11, 1943
Wahoo (SS-238)
Eighty men lost
Sunk by aerial bombs

October 12, 1943
Dorado (SS-248)
Seventy-six men lost
Sunk by friendly aircraft

November 16, 1943
Corvina (SS-226)
Eighty-two men lost
Sunk by enemy submarine

November 19, 1943
Sculpin (SS-191)
Sixty-three men lost, twenty-one survivors
taken prisoner
Sunk by surface craft

November 23, 1943
Capelin (SS-289)
Seventy-eight men lost
Sunk by surface craft

January 5, 1944
Scorpion (SS-278)
Seventy-six men lost
Sunk by enemy mines

February 26, 1944
Grayback (SS-208)
Eighty men lost
Sunk by surface craft and aerial bombs

February 29, 1944
Trout (SS-202)
Eight-one men lost
Sunk by surface craft

March 26, 1944
Tullibee (SS-284)
Seventy-nine men lost, one survivor taken prisoner
Sunk by own torpedo

April 7, 1944
Gudgeon (SS-211)
Seventy-eight men lost
Sunk by surface craft and aerial bombs

June 1, 1944
Herring (SS-233)
Eighty-four men lost
Sunk by surface craft

June 14, 1944
Golet (SS-361)
Eight-two men lost
Sunk by surface craft

July 4, 1944
S-28 (SS-133)
Fifty-two men lost
Sunk cause unknown

July 26, 1944
Robalo (SS-273)
Seventy-seven lost, four survived as POWs but came home
Sunk by enemy mines

August 13, 1944
Flier (SS-250)
Seventy-eight men lost, eight survivors
Sunk by enemy mines

August 24, 1944
Harder (SS-257)
Seventy-nine men lost
Sunk by surface craft

October 3, 1944
Seawolf (SS-197)
Seventy-nine men lost
Sunk by friendly fire

October 17, 1944
Escolar (SS-294)
Eight men lost
Sunk by enemy mines

October 24, 1944
Darter (SS-227)
No loss of life
Ran aground

October 24, 1944
Shark II (SS-314)
Eighty-seven men lost
Sunk by surface craft

October 25, 1944
Tang (SS-306)
Seventy-eight men lost, nine survivors
taken prisoner
Sunk by own torpedo

November 7, 1944
Albacore (SS-218)
Eighty-six men lost
Sunk by enemy mines

November 8, 1944
Growler (SS-215)
Eighty-five men lost
Sunk cause unknown

November 9, 1944
Scamp (SS-277)
Eight-three men lost
Sunk by surface craft and
aerial bombs

January 12, 1945
Swordfish (SS-193)
Eighty-five men lost
Sunk cause unknown

February 4, 1945
Barbel (SS-316)
Eighty-one men lost
Sunk by aerial bombs

March 20, 1945
Kete (SS-369)
Eighty-seven men lost
Sunk cause unknown

March 26, 1945
Trigger (SS-237)
Eighty-nine men lost
Sunk by surface craft and aerial bombs

April 8, 1945
Trigger (SS-279)
Eighty-four men lost
Sunk cause unknown

May 3, 1945
Lagarto (SS-371)
Eighty-five men lost
Sunk by surface craft

June 18, 1945
Bonefish (SS-223)
Eighty-five men lost
Sunk by surface craft

August 6, 1945
Bullhead (SS-332)
Eighty-four men lost
Sunk by aerial bombs

"Mentality in Submarines"
Reprinted with permission from the magazine *Polaris* / September 2014

Men selected for submarine duty have to be screened to cope with the mental and emotional experiences they will encounter. The tension, heat, silent running, the long hours at battle stations, and the feeling of helplessness against enemy depth bombs and depth charge attacks often strained the sanity of the best of them. One out of seventy-five submarine men break temporarily during battle. Sleeping and eating for half the crew often become a chore for days after a harrowing experience. Sometimes shipmates, when becoming hysterical, had to be held down, even given a shot to knock them out. On one submarine, a radioman went off, pulling wires out in the radio shack. He had to be tranquilized and was strapped in his bunk for days. Often gunners strafing the enemy with gunfire would vomit, have insomnia, nightmares or anxiety attacks and be stressed out for days. Some would stare into space in a catatonic state, their minds coping with it by blanking-out. Others would try to commit suicide, to end it before it ended them. There are accounts of two submariners actually taking their own lives—one on board and another refusing to go to sea who hung himself in the barracks with a buffer cord.

To avoid such cases, which have a demoralizing effect on the crew, the submarine service created a tight method of screening out men who could possibly be unable to mentally handle adverse conditions. Naval Submarine Base New London, the United States Navy's primary East Coast submarine base, also known as the "Home of the Submarine Force," is located in Groton, Connecticut. It set the standard for detecting the strengths and weaknesses of Navy personnel. First, the Navy doctors agreed, the emotionally mature volunteer made the most levelheaded submarine man. After interviewing thousands of volunteers, they made a list of danger signals which pointed to instability. Trick psychological tests were administered to exclude weaker men in areas such as: abnormal shyness (inability to take initiative/command/perform under duress) or sensitivity (unable to take criticism/instruction or bear the senses of pain, stress, or suffering), difficulty in school (hard to train or follow rules), truancy (punctuality/schedules/duty times) and dislike of teachers (leaders, authority), fear of lightning or of the dark, fear of elevators or crowded spaces (indicating claustrophobia), shunning of girls after puberty (an indication of gender preference, which would adversely affect morale), abnormal attachment to mother (an indication of Oedipus Complex or co-dependence), not liking discipline (structure/consistency over long periods of time), not liking competitive games that could cause injury (fear of losing or pain), stammering (clear communication is essential to survival in the military), and religious fanaticism. (Lack of tolerance for others' beliefs or discrimination/prejudice for others is detrimental to camaraderie, especially when in prolonged confinement.)

Mothers of Navy men often put heavy pressure on their sons to withdraw from submarine training. Some mothers were interviewed by Navy doctors, and if they found the son was unduly influenced by her fears, he was usually dropped from training.

When a man or woman enlists in the Navy, he or she is interviewed by a Navy psychiatrist. Volunteers for submarines are then interviewed a second time by a specialized psychiatrist, one who is stricter in selection for submarine duty. Some of the mental health professionals found that teenagers often could not measure up to the maturity requirements for service in submarines. In many cases, the Navy refused to accept men under nineteen for submarine duty. Those men who wished to serve beneath the waves were picked from the top half of the Navy's intelligence scale, as well as individuals in top physical condition.

Despite this pre-screening, up to 30 percent were turned away after careful psychiatrist examination.

After war patrols, especially where crews felt high tension during battle stations, submarine men were assigned rest periods (R&R—rest and recovery) to recuperate from the strain. Among others, there was the Royal Hawaiian Hotel and the rest camps in Australia and Midway Island where they could breathe fresh air, sleep in a real bed, and see sunshine for a week or two while their boat was being outfitted for another war patrol.

With this benevolent program, the submarine service ended with one of the lowest psychiatric rates in the armed forces. From the 1,520 war patrols, only sixty-two serious psychoneurotic cases developed. One of these five was psychotic.

H. L. Hunley

H. L. Hunley, named for her inventor, Horace Lawson Hunley, was a hand-powered submarine of the Confederate States of America. She was the first combat submarine to sink a warship while not completely submerged and, following her successful attack, was lost along with her crew before she could return to base. The Confederacy lost twenty-one crewmen in three sinkings of the *Hunley* during her short career.

Finally located in 1995, the *Hunley* was raised in 2000 and is on display in North Charleston, South Carolina, at the Warren Lasch Conservation Center on the Cooper River.

Information taken from https://en.wikipedia.org/wiki/H._L._Hunley_(submarine)

"Tossing Lines: Hats Off to All Submariners"

Written by John Steward

Reprinted from *The Day*, April 7, 2015[1]

Here in the Submarine Capitol of the World, submariners are who we are. Whether we build them, serve on them or just catch a glimpse of one now and then gliding on the Thames River, subs have always been a part of our lives.

Active and retired Navy personnel and the extended families of Electric Boat shipbuilders fill communities throughout Connecticut and Rhode Island. Newspapers cover submarines returning to the Sub Base in Groton after long deployments.

That is why, when I first laid eyes on an eerie x-ray of the confederate submarine *H.L. Hunley* on CNN.com, I felt a connection to those skeletons trapped inside because every submariner is one of our own.

The *Hunley* sank in 1864 after fatally torpedoing the USS *Housatonic* off the coast of South Carolina. The *Hunley* was recovered in 2000 and underwent archaeological processing in a lab.

Powered by hand, the heavy sub's seven crank handle positions were painstakingly excavated from the sediment. One by one, each skeleton was exposed at his station. They had never moved.

Time and the ocean stole skin, muscle and tissue but left the skeletons remarkably preserved. Some still wore shoes.

Mainstream media avoided the crew's remains but these men had names. The website for *Friends of the Hunley* (friendsofthehunley.org) tells their story.

Inside the sub, personal effects, small symbols of humanity, had settled in place as their owners slowly disintegrated—shoes,

---

[1] http://www.theday.com/article/20150407/NWS01/150409492

wood and brass buttons, a tin canteen, a wallet, a wooden pipe for smoking and bits of clothing.

In the front of the boat still on station beneath the forward conning tower sat the skeleton of Lt. George E. Dixon, the *Hunley's* commander. He fired the torpedo that sunk the *Housatonic*, introducing submarines to naval warfare.

Jewelry and an ornate gold watch mingled with his bones. A healed gunshot wound was found in Dixon's left upper thigh. He had become legend for the $20 gold good luck piece that once deflected the bullet, saving his leg. Dixon carried it that night.

At the first crank were the bones of twenty-year-old Arnold Becker. His teeth showed signs of childhood illness or occasional malnutrition. His skeleton still held signs of strain from turning the crank shaft.

Still manning the second crank were the remains of a man named Lumpkin, first name undetermined. In his early forties, he showed past evidence of a broken nose, cheek and foot. He had notches in his teeth where he held his smoking pipe. His sewing kit and pocketknife lay with his bones.

Frank Collins was the tallest skeleton, collapsed at the third crank handle. Collins had "tailor notches" in his teeth from working with metal needles. He apprenticed in his grandfather's cobbler shop.

The bones of J. F. Carlsen, in his early twenties, rested at the fourth crank handle. Carlsen had survived a mutiny, testifying in an 1861 treason trial in Charleston.

Details are sketchy about a man named Miller, manning the fifth position. He was one of the oldest, in his mid-forties. His skeleton spoke of a hard physical life, showing old fractures on his rib, leg and skull. He was a heavy smoker with a touch of arthritis.

At the sixth crank sat James A. Wicks, father of four girls. A heavy tobacco user with light brown hair and blue eyes, seven U.S. Navy buttons mingled with his bones.

Nestled at the seventh crank position was Joseph Ridgaway, just over thirty. Scattered among his bones was a slouch hat and pencil. Mysteriously, around his neck hung the dog tag of Connecticut soldier Ezra Chamberlin, who died at the Battle of Morris Island where Ridgaway had also fought.

In 2004, the *Hunley* crew was buried amid great fanfare in Charleston, S.C., laid to rest as they had died—side-by-side.

Ted Dubay of East Lyme, submariner and author of *Three Knots to Nowhere: A Cold War Submariner on the Undersea Frontline*, wrote: "All submarines operate on the edge of survivability."

The courage it took to man the hand-cranked *Hunley* is no different than the courage it takes to man today's sophisticated nuclear submarines. The deep, unforgiving sea hasn't changed.

Hats off to all submariners.

* * *

John Steward can be reached at tossinglines@gmail.com.

USS *Thresher* (SS-200)

The **USS *Thresher* (SS-200)** was a *Tambor*-class submarine that was commissioned on 27 August, 1940, and finally decommissioned on 12 July, 1946. For her service, she received fifteen battle stars and a Navy Unit Commendation, making her one of the most highly decorated US ships of World War II.

Information taken from https://en.wikipedia.org/wiki/USS_Thresher_(SS-200)

BILLY A. GRIEVES

Information submitted by Billy A. Grieves to Mary Nida Smith

Bill Grieves joined the Navy in 1939. While he was in boot camp, the submarine USS *Squalus* (SS-192) went down off the coast of New Hampshire. He was one of twelve volunteers sent north to assist in raising the *Squalus*. When they finally brought it to the surface, twenty-six bodies were aboard, only half of her crew. They towed her into the Navy yard at Portsmouth. While working on the salvage operation, he became keenly interested in submarines and the men who manned them. Grieves was determined to become a submariner.

His first assignment was the USS *R10*, an old school boat at the submarine base at New London, Connecticut. For the first three months, he focused all his energy on qualifying for his submarine dolphins. "I was eighteen when I put on my uniform. It was the proudest day of my life," said Grieves. School boat duty did not appeal to him. He wanted to ride a submarine above and below the seas to the other side of the world.

He requested assignment to new construction, and he was transferred to the USS *Thresher* (SS-200). The boat was commissioned in August 1940. It went under diving and running trials to test the boat's capabilities. At the same time, the new crew was tested during training. Later, they joined the fleet at Pearl Harbor, in early 1941.

On October 21, 1941, the *Thresher* put out to sea on what they thought was just another training mission. Their assignment was to conduct a forty-eight-day simulated war patrol protecting the northern approaches to the Island of Midway.

They were to maintain radio silence and remain submerged throughout the daylight hours, surfacing only after dark to charge batteries. They were to keep two torpedo tubes—fore and aft—ready to fire at all times. If any offensive action was taken against Midway, they were to sink anything in sight.

Four days later they arrived on station, where they commenced diving each day—all day long. "I hated it. Tedious days lapsed into monotonous weeks. Fresh provisions ran out. Dehydrated substitutes were used. Bland and unappetizing food was placed on our menu. We saved freshwater for cooking and drinking. Showers ceased as the primitive waste-boat evaporators struggled inefficiently to keep up with the demand. I wondered how many more days we could survive like this," said Grieves.

On December 4, after forty consecutive all-day dives—food, fuel, and freshwater critically low—a sudden relief swept through the boat. The captain, Commander William Anderson, announced that the USS *Trout* had arrived to relieve them.

They turned *Thresher's* bow eastward toward Oahu, running into angry seas with enormous waves and heavy winds. The bow continued to plunge into the swell as the water covered the conning tower, cascading over the bridge and periscope shears. During one of the immersions, Seaman Bill Grover, the port lookout, was washed from his perch high on the shears onto the small deck on the after end of the conning tower known as the "cigarette" deck.

The captain ordered a couple of the crew to carry Grover below to his (the captain's) bunk. He was in extensive pain with a broken femur and a fractured skull. Someone had to stay with him at all times. Doc Millis, the pharmacist mate, maintained an around-the-clock vigil. Millis mentioned that Grover talked of home and made unusual predictions.

It was December 7, 1941, the day they were to make port at Pearl Harbor. The announcement came over the speakers that the Japanese had attacked Pearl. As they approached Oahu, the air and surface contacts increased. The captain never was given time to establish identification. All submarines were enemies.

Orders came that the minefields around the channel had been activated. They were given a location to meet with the destroyer USS *Litchfield*. She was to escort them through the mines and channel. They had sighted her, but she must have identified them wrong, as she ran off leaving them unaided.

Approaching the minefield submerged, they sighted another four-stack destroyer, which they thought was the *Litchfield*. Captain Anderson ordered a recognition transmitted by sonar. They also sent up a smoke flare from periscope depth. The gunners aboard the destroyer took bearings on the flare. "Just as we broke the surface, all hell broke loose. We heard machine gun fire, and at the same time a five-inch shell whistled across our blow. A row of dents laced the conning tower. We were in a flooded condition as we dove to 287 feet in thirty-seven seconds," said Grieves. "That night our minds were not on the attack, but on our fellow crew member, Bill Grover. He died as Doc Millis provided comfort the best he knew how."

The night was spent evading "friendly" forces. The following day they successfully made connection with the destroyer USS *Thornton*. It arrived to escort the *Thresher* safely into Pearl Harbor. Upon entering Pearl Harbor, they were greeted with the first evidence of the attack, the USS *Nevada* beached at the mouth of the channel. Rounding the bend, the USS *Oglala* appeared capsized on her port side. "But, the two ships didn't prepare us for the shock of what came next," said Billy. "As we neared the Navy Yard, a cloud of heavy, dense, gray smoke blotted out the Hawaiian sun. The smoke hung low, and the strong odor of burning oil was everywhere. As we moved in closer, we saw the battleships: the *Oklahoma* was capsized and keel up, the *Arizona* was on the bottom, and the *California*, *West Virginia*, *Tennessee*, and the *Maryland* were all heavily damaged."

They slowly continued by Battleship Row as the bow sliced through the layer of thick oil covering the water like a large black blanket of death. "Almost everyone was standing on deck. Silently we stared out, filling our souls with overwhelming rage. Gone were the exhaustion, frustration, and the monotony of our six weeks at sea. At that moment, we were ready to turn around and head back to sea to seek retribution," said Billy Grieves. His voice rose in anger as his eyes became moist.

The Japanese swept across the Pacific, striking Pearl Harbor, a few days later striking Manila. This left the American Navy in a shambles. The battleships either rested on the bottom or were badly damaged.

During their two weeks' shore duty following the bombing of Pearl Harbor, life at the Royal Hawaiian Hotel on Waikiki Beach changed constantly. Stretched out along the beaches were coils of barbed wire in four to five rows. Martial law ruled the islands. Every bar and nightclub was closed. At six o'clock, curfew was strictly enforced and the island had orders for no lights at night— a total "blackout." No air conditioners. It was hot and muggy.

Every woman who wasn't a resident of the island was shipped back to the States aboard the carriers *Lurine, Mariposa,* and the *Monterey.*

It was easy to tell a return sailor after about sixty days below the surface of the sea. He usually had long hair, was unshaven, and his skin was pale white. Sailors stood out, as they never traveled alone.

A state of panic reigned in Pearl Harbor after the Japanese attack. Everyone was "trigger happy." They fired first and asked questions later. Many of our boats putting out or coming in to Pearl came under attack by our own military. Some were damaged, and they had to go in for repairs.

During this time a relief crew boarded the *Thresher* to repair the damage and refit. (Refit meant repairing any damage to prepare for another patrol.) When the crew returned to board, their job was to take on torpedoes, fuel, freshwater, and food.

On December 30, 1941, they departed from Pearl Harbor on their second war patrol to the Marshall and Mariana islands. Later they sailed to investigate several other islands. They were assigned off the waters of Guam, which was being held by the Japanese. In the early morning of February 4, they arrived but spent little time near Guam, because of overwhelming dangers of anti-submarine warfare. On February 26, they returned to Pearl Harbor to await their next orders.

The third war patrol began on April 10, 1942, with Commander Bill Anderson as the new skipper. "We arrived off Tokyo

Bay when, through his periscope, the skipper sighted a freighter with one destroyer coming out of the channel. We approached and fired one fish with the torpedo depth set to pass beneath the keel. When the magnetic exploder detonated the warhead, the Japanese 3,039-ton *Sado Maru* was blown into sections, and it sank in two minutes. The destroyer following the torpedo wake was right on top of them," Grieves related.

"The first depth charges were close aboard the stern, driving us down 410 feet. Hanging as if suspended, the planesmen fought to regain lost trim. Slowly the boat rose to 350 feet. The sea pressure decreased as the hull cracked loudly in regaining its configuration. The severe concussion had knocked the port propeller shaft out of alignment, causing the boat to fishtail wildly, sending loud vibrations throughout the rooms. In the torpedo room, cans of food stowed behind the reload torpedoes broke loose, crashing against the reload racks. A heavy wrench in the engine room, suspended on the side of a locker, thumped loudly against it. In every compartment the crew tried to eliminate the noises. When the power was placed on the port shaft, the noise was almost intolerable. Without the port screw, depth control was impossible. Two more destroyers joined in the hunt.

"In the hours that followed, the destroyers trailed tenaciously. When we tried to come up past 300 feet, depth charges drove us back down. Close to midnight, after fourteen hours under attack and eighteen hours submerged, the oxygen was dangerously low. We were breathing in deep, rapid gasps. The batteries were in a critical state. A feeling of hopelessness settled over the crew.

"Captain Anderson decided to try his last tactic. He ordered a 180° turn to head toward Tokyo, followed by 'full surface.' Under the darkest of night we were able to lose our enemies," stated Grieves.

On June 26, the fourth war patrol started. The *Thresher* had just come out of dry dock after undergoing extensive repairs from damages sustained on the last run. Their skipper, Commander William L. Anderson, was relieved and sent back to the States. The new skipper was Commander William J. Millican, a short, stocky, aggressive man. He had been a champion boxer at the Naval Academy. "As we got to know him, every crew member would willingly follow him anywhere," said Grieves.

"The old 'four-pipe' destroyer, USS *Litchfield*, escorted us as we followed closely in her wake. Slowly we traveled over mines through the channel to open water by Midway Island and the International Date Line, before we arrived at the Marshall Islands near Maloelap."

On the first day, July 6, Commander Millican sighted a four-ship convoy coming through the channel. The last ship was a tanker. "We had orders from COMSUBPAC to sink tankers first. Fuel was very important to Japan. We allowed the first three to pass by. Then, we fired two fish at the tanker. It was a HIT! She burst into flame and sank in about two minutes. By dang! A Japanese airplane and the escort ship arrived on the scene. We suddenly dove deeper to silent running," said Grieves. "In the next three hours we received nineteen depth charges." Later, the escort departed to return to protect its convoy.

The next day they approached the island of Kwajalein through Gea Pass. The Pass was wide and deep, a good place to maneuver a submarine in time of battle. The first day on duty, the captain sighted several ships through his periscope, including three "I Boats" (Japanese submarines). None came within torpedo range. That night they surfaced to charge the batteries while they stayed in the Pass.

It was not quite dawn, and the batteries were charged. The cooks had just finished baking, and the ovens were cooling.

"We dove before sunrise at about 0800 hours. The captain raised the periscope for his regular sweep. A flash of light blinded him. He could see it was a new ship—first time out and her deck was lined with Japanese sailors in white uniforms. It was the 4,836-ton Motor Torpedo Boat Tender, *Shinsho Maru*, and it was without escorts.

"As it cruised within their range, we were ordered to make tubes three and four ready to fire. I had the starboard where I went to work on number three. My buddy, Charlie Fry, made ready number four. When ready, we raised the ready-to-fire levers to give the signal in the conning tower. As the target angle approached zero, the captain ordered, 'Final bearing and shoot! Up scope!' He zeroed the periscope on the target, checked the overhead azimuth, and then he ordered, 'Stand by three! Fire three! Fire four!'" recalled Grieves, as if it were today. The boat vibrated as they listened in silence, as the fish sped down the track.

"The torpedoes were not set to strike the target, but to pass beneath. The exploder on the Mark XIV torpedo contained a magnetic feature, so when it passed within the magnetic proximity of its hull it would detonate the warhead at the ship's most vulnerable point, her keel.

"The wait was short as the range was under a thousand yards. BOOM! Followed by another BOOM! Two hits. It blew the bow off the ship, followed by blowing off the stern. Within minutes it sank below the surface in a huge cloud of steam. Suddenly the water around us was covered with white uniforms.

"Survivors meant the enemy. Their military force would be arriving to pick them up. So would the *Thresher*. We were cruising slowly at periscope depth. The scope was down and the boat was silent. Suddenly the loudest violent explosion we had ever heard went right beneath our bow. It was an airplane carrying depth charges.

"The bow erupted with such violence that the men sitting on the bunks were lifted out of them. Men standing back aft were thrown to the deck. Charlie and I grabbed on to the tubes and hung on for our lives," said Grieves. The captain's orders followed immediately, "All ahead full! Depth 300! All compartments check for damage."

Grieves checked the starboard bank and the bilge, while Charlie checked the port bank. The other guys checked the pitometer log well and the sound heads—no damage. Each department phoned in "no damage"—so they thought.

What they didn't know was that the Mark XIV torpedo, which weighed 3,421 pounds and left the tube at forty-seven knots, received its impetus from 400 pounds of air stored in impulse bottles located in the superstructure above the tubes. When the charge went off, the seal to number-one impulse bottle was cracked. Because of this, the *Thresher* was laying a stream of bubbles on the surface. They were down 300 feet and the depth charges continued. Sonar picked up the sound of three sets of screws.

"Unfailingly, the destroyer homed in on our wake. The captain tried to get the *Thresher* out of the channel and into the ocean. The depth charges continued. Then, suddenly, the destroyer stopped. We knew they had a fix on our position and our depth, yet the sea was quiet. The unbelievable silence continued," declared Grieves.

"The silence was broken by a loud 'clanking' echo that moved aft down the starboard side of the hull. The message, 'For'd room to control, we are experiencing a loud clanking noise moving aft down the stab'rd side,' was repeated by each department. Suddenly . . . it was gone. I thought, *Now what?*" said Grieves.

It was the planesmen who discovered they were in trouble. The stem, the back end of the submarine, was rising substantially. Bubbles continued to rise, and there was nothing to do about it. To their amazement they came to the realization that the starboard stern plane guard had been hooked by a huge grapnel. It was slowly pulling them up—stem first.

The captain's first order was to pour more power to the screws. The *Thresher* and the crew were fighting for their lives. When the power hit the screws, the boat began to vibrate in an uncontrolled shaking. It changed nothing. They were still hooked. The captain ordered all stop. With such an extreme measure of increase and shut down, the batteries would not last long. The next order the captain gave was to add more weight to the stem. The orders continued, as the captain tried everything. After the trim tank was filled with water from the sea, the after WRT tank was flooded, and then the after torpedo room bilges were flooded to the deck plate. The boat took on tons of ballast (weight) to keep it from rising. From 300 feet, they were up to 250 feet.

"The captain had tried everything. It was the end," said Grieves. "It was apparent that we would lose our boat, for it was passing 100 feet upward. The enemy was pulling us to the top. The captain immediately gave orders to the radiomen to demolish all decoding equipment. The sledgehammers were brought out. The pounding could be heard echoing in every nook of the boat. The gunners mate and crew in the torpedo received orders to position the demolition charges for scuttling—to destroy the boat and all aboard.

"Each torpedo room carried a fifty-five-pound charge of TNT. It would be placed between the warheads of the re-load torpedoes. When the order came to detonate, it would obliterate both compartments and hopefully the shit pulling us up. No one objected as the crew members went about their business. Some of the men bowed their heads in prayer. Wes Headington stood up and walked over to me with outstretched hands. I slowly got up as we shook hands. We peered deep into each other's eyes. Not a word was spoken," said Grieves.

"We waited for what felt like hours of apprehension, when the crew received another order. The captain had one more desperate maneuver to try. He ordered forward trim flooded from the after trim. The down angle, already steep, became steeper as he ordered, 'Left full rudder! All ahead emergency!' The power hit the screws with a shudder. The boat heaved slightly into a port list, and suddenly we were freed from the grapnel's hooks and heading for the bottom at high speed."

"Blow bow buoyancy!" ordered the captain. As 3,000 pounds of air hit the forward tank, the bow heaved upward, saving the boat from hitting the bottom. The crew instantly went into action, pumping tons of ballast and blowing it overboard. The submarine remained at 300 feet until, under the darkness of night, they evaded the enemy and surfaced. The *Thresher* had taken forty-one depth charges. The patrol continued past Truk Atoll, Yap, and Palau, and turned south across the equator through the Dutch East Indies to the Indian Ocean, before arriving in port at Freemantle, West Australia.

"Captain CDR Bill Millican stayed for four more runs on the USS *Thresher* before he was transferred to the States to command the USS *Escolar*, a new submarine. He earned two Navy Crosses for the ships we sank. He took several of the *Thresher* shipmates with him. The *Escolar* went on their first war patrol to the coast of China off the Yellow Sea. We learned of their arrival, but that was the last message. A message that was so familiar followed: Overdue and presumed lost. Nothing was heard of them again. We were deeply saddened."

* * *

Billy Grieves TM 1/c was in charge of the forward torpedo aboard the USS *Thresher* (SS-200) during eleven war patrols. He was awarded the Submarine Combat medal and two Bronze

Star medals. The *Thresher* received fifteen battle stars and a Navy Unit Commendation for World War II. Grieves served two war patrols aboard USS *Lizardfish* (SS- 373). He was honorably discharged from the Navy on October 10, 1945, after serving six and a half years. Billy served twenty-seven years with the Detroit Fire Department, retiring as lieutenant. He continued to work as an industrial firefighter with the Ford Motor Company for ten years. He and his wife, the former Muriel Jeanne Bach, married in 1947, raised two daughters, and as of this writing they resided in Sun City West, Arizona.

Below is how Bill Grieves and many, many men feel today:

"Forget Pearl Harbor? Never! One step aboard the memorial erected over the hull of the USS *Arizona*, and you are reminded that 1,100 young American sailors are still entombed beneath our feet. At this time you feel no peace of mind, for it is shattered for days with the feeling of rage. Once you have been placed in the horrors of war, it never leaves you."

USS *Guitarro* (SS-363)

USS *Guitarro* (SS-363) was a *Balao*-class submarine that was commissioned on 26 January, 1944. She was awarded four battle stars and a Navy Unit Commendation for her World War II service.

Information taken from https://en.wikipedia.org/wiki/USS_ Guitarro_(SS-363)

JAMES A. DAVIDSON

Information submitted by James A. Davidson to Mary Nida Smith

James A. Davidson's submarine career was started by accident when his draft board said they were going to call him into the military service in a week. He had applied to join the Marine Corps because he liked the fancy looking red stripe on their uniform. But then he heard that if he could pass the Navy typing test, he could come into the Navy at sixty dollars a month instead of the normal twenty-five dollars. He took the test and passed it. He was sworn into the Navy reserve as a V-6 for the duration of the emergency.

On October 21, 1941, Davidson reported to the receiving station at the Philadelphia Naval Shipyard in Pennsylvania. He said he had nothing else better to do, so he volunteered. He and his co-volunteers removed screens on the barracks, stored them, helped handle lines to move big ships, and marched in a parade in Philadelphia.

He doesn't remember volunteering for submarine duty. If he had his choice he would have picked a battleship in Pearl Harbor, because the United States had a big investment there, and Hawaii would always be an interesting place to be. He was told to report to New London.

When Davidson arrived, he noticed lots of submarines. Someone asked the group, "Who would like to go to Key West, Florida?" He thought that sounded great. It was late November, 1941. It was starting to feel like winter, and he had never been to Florida.

On November 18, 1941, Davidson reported to Chief Yeoman McLean in Key West, who assigned him to the USS *R-2* submarine, the flag sub for the Submarine Division Twelve. The *R-2* was a World War I submarine. The Chief Yeoman referred to him as a V-6 troublemaker and freshwater sailor, because he outranked many of the yeoman strikers and he was already in the Atlantic fleet.

"I liked it there. I typed in Building 1010, where yeoman stayed," said Davidson. "I got paid twice a month, plus I started receiving hazardous duty pay. The roller skating rink and the USO were both outside the gate. I had no complaints, as I never went to boot camp, submarine school, or yeoman's school."

By December 7, 1941, Davidson had earned two medals: the American Defense medal with a Fleet clasp and the American Theater Medal. Davidson decided to attend night school at the Convent of Mary Immaculate, where he received his certificate.

On August 1, 1942, he passed the test and was promoted to Yeoman Second Class. Davidson escorted Commander Gorry of the Submarine Division Twelve on practice trips to sea on various R-type submarines, Eagle boats, and WWI destroyers, usually the USS *Dahlgren*, a WWI submarine.

"I carried his binoculars and various books. My arms were always full, which made it difficult to ride as I bounced around in small motor whale boats traveling from ship to ship. We spent most of our time on the target as submarines shot dummy torpedoes under us," said Davidson.

On June 17, he was transferred to the submarine USS *R-10*. His commanding officer was E. D. Haskins, an Annapolis graduate. The commander was then transferred to "New Construction," where in Manitowoc, Wisconsin, he took command of the new USS *Guitarro* (SS-365) submarine. Davidson's job was to have Haskins's orders and laundry ready to send with him. Later Haskins was replaced by Officer George Sharp.

On November 1, 1943, Davidson was eligible to take another test through which he qualified in submarines on USS *R-10* on January 3, 1944. He had to make drawings and stand watch at various stations out at sea to qualify.

In February 1944, he was transferred to the USS *Icefish* in Manitowoc, Wisconsin, and was looking forward to shore duty. Meanwhile, the USS *Guitarro* was preparing to leave. The crew had their party and pictures taken. They set sail into the lake, but made a mistake as they were diving. The conning tower hatch was open. When the men in the control room below saw the water coming in, they instantly closed the hatch. "First Class Yeoman McAndrews in the conning tower got caught up to his waist in frigid cold water before the problem was corrected," recounted Davidson as he recalled a story someone had told him.

Captain Haskins said he needed a new yeoman. He told Davidson he didn't have to wait for the USS *Icefish*. He could come aboard in a couple of days as his new yeoman.

"I was reluctant, as I wanted my shore duty. I asked if I could go home to see my family while they traveled down the Mississippi, and I would meet them in New Orleans. To my surprise, the captain said 'Yes.'" On February 12, 1944, Davidson transferred from the USS *Icefish* to the *Guitarro*.

While he was home, he explained to his parents that so far, his submarine duty had not been dangerous, and that each crew member was a volunteer. To his surprise and disappointment, his parents didn't discourage him from being a submariner. But Davidson questioned this part of his career; he didn't want to be placed in harm's way or to die. Nevertheless, he did like the pay.

At New Orleans some of the crew opted out. When they got to Panama, a few more dropped out. At Pearl Harbor, the last ones were transferred. "I wondered," Davidson said, "if this is the way there were relief crews." At Midway they topped off with fuel. They crossed the 180 meridian at latitude 28 N at 0430, and were on their first war patrol. If he recalled correctly, they sank their first Japanese merchant ship on May 30, 1944. Each time, they were heavily depth charged. They were operating between Formosa and China in the Taiwan Strait and calling themselves "The Galloping Ghosts of Formosa Coast."

"We crossed the equator at longitude 126, 30' E at 2213 on June 13, 1944, and I became a 'shellback,'" Richardson remarked proudly.

After they ran out of torpedoes and almost out of fuel, the captain pulled into Darwin, Australia. The Japanese had already been there. Darwin was bombed flat except for the bank vault. Everywhere there were ships upside down in the harbor. Fortunately, they had enough fuel to continue to Fremantle, Southwestern Australia. On June 27, 1944, they completed a fifty-one-day successful war patrol. They were finally able to come out of the hatches to see daylight and spend two weeks' recovery time in nearby Perth.

"Although we claimed three ships totaling 21,300 tons, only two ships totaling 11,200 tons were confirmed. The captain received a Navy Cross, and the crew received a submarine combat patrol pin," said Davidson, a little disappointed that they couldn't confirm the third ship.

Their second successful war patrol lasted forty-eight days in the South China Sea. It was completed on September 24, 1944. They claimed 3.5 ships totaling 32,700 tons, with two ships totaling 10,999 tons confirmed. Captain Haskins received his third Navy Cross and the crew received a Navy Unit Commendation and a second gold star for their combat pin. They received no credit for their hits on a Japanese cruiser that was on its way to the battle of Layte Gulf.

They had seen another Japanese cruiser, but were unable to get close enough for a shot so they reported its course. The next one was already damaged, so they ran under the destroyer escorts, firing seven torpedoes, resulting in three hits. The escorts figured where they were, but they didn't drop depth charges the first time over them. While the escorts turned around, the *Guitarro* dropped 300 feet.

"I was on the battle phones as usual in the control room," Davidson said. "This time the depth charges were coming right at us. The captain said a blue flash came through the conning tower hatch as all lights went out. I could hear a loud hissing sound in the pump room below me. The forward and after torpedo rooms both reported leaks. I really thought it was all over for us. Finally, the lights came back on and we got the leaks stopped. Again, we received no credit for the cruiser that went aground and was finished by our aircraft. Thank God for our planes."

After they returned to their base port, the Navy started rotating the crew. Davidson and other crew members got off. Davidson was now a Chief Yeoman. He was assigned on December 24 to be private secretary for Captain Huffman, commander of Submarine Squadron 26, on board the submarine tender USS *Anthedon* at Fremantle. They then continued up to Subic Bay in the Philippines, where Captain Huffman was replaced by Captain Becon until the war ended.

"By September 16, 1945, I was shipped to Commander Submarine Administration at Mare Island, California. On December 17, 1945, I received an honorable discharge in Sampson, New York, as Chief Yeoman (SS), but I continued to have a long navel career on the USS *Canopus*, USS *Permit*, and others."

* * *

As of 2005, James A Davidson YNC (SS) USN-RET lived in Gulfport, Mississippi. At one time, he reported, "In Gulfport we were right in the center of Hurricane Katrina. From my room on the fifth floor, I watched the water rise and the trees blow over. Then automobiles started to float around the parking lots. I was totally secure, except we had no electricity or water, so about six buses evacuated us all with police escort out of Gulfport to Washington, D.C. No one was allowed back. It may take years to restore. There are over one thousand military retirees here in D.C."

Davidson retired from the Navy at age fifty-eight and received his pension at sixty as a CWO-4. Davidson married Rosalie (Hensley) Russell in Ashland, Kentucky, May 18, 1946. As of this writing, they have seven children and twelve grandchildren.

USS *Perch* (SS-176)

USS *Perch* (SS-176), the lead ship of *Perch*-class submarines of the United States Navy, was commissioned on November 19, 1936. On March 3, 1942, she embarked on an unsuccessful test dive and was attacked by two Japanese cruisers soon afterward. Her entire crew of fifty-nine men was captured by the Japanese and placed in POW camps. Only five survived to return to the United States. Her wreck was discovered off the coast of Java in 2006 on Thanksgiving Day.

Information taken from https://en.wikipedia.org/wiki/USS_Perch_(SS-176)

ROBERT WAYNE LENTS (FORMER POW)

From a brief article on the USS *Perch* (formerly P-5) by Robert Wayne Lents[2]

Robert Wayne Lents, who turned ninety-three-years-old in 2015, was one of sixty-three crew members aboard the USS *Perch* who was reported missing in action. He spent three and a half years as a

---

[2] From the book *U.S. Submarine Veterans of World War II*, Volume Three (Taylor Publishing Company).

USS *Perch* (SS-176),
Robert Lents, POW

Japanese prisoner of war, upon release weighing eighty pounds. He is a member of the USSVI Twin Lakes Base, Mountain Home, Arkansas. He and his wife of sixty-nine years recently moved to Arkansas Veterans Home in Fayetteville, Arkansas.

The USS *Perch* (SS-176) was the first American submarine sunk by the Japanese. In 2010, Torpedoman Third Class Lents believed he was one of only five surviving members. Before the *Perch*, Lents was aboard the USS *Seawolf* (SS-195) that disappeared off Manus Island, New Guinea. Lents was known as the only remaining crew member from the USS *Seawolf* (WWII).

Lents and other World War II prisoners have been invited to be part of the Japanese/POW Friendship Program. The American Defenders of *Bataan* and *Corregidor*, along with the U.S. Department of State, have been working to identify former POWs.

MARIAN "TURK" TURNER (FORMER POW)

"World War II POW, Submarine Remembered"

Written by Kevin Copeland, Commander

Submarine Force Atlantic Public Affairs, March 7, 2011

NORFOLK, Virginia. (NNS)—The life of a World War II submariner and POW was celebrated and remembered during a funeral in Virginia Beach, Virginia, March 5.

Marion "Turk" Turner passed away February 28 after a lengthy illness. He was a retired submariner who survived three and half years in a Japanese prisoner of war (POW) camp during World War II.

A longtime resident of Virginia Beach, Virginia, Turner was born in Moultrie, Georgia, on April 22, 1918.

Turner enlisted in the Navy on October 12, 1939, and elected to serve on submarines as an Electrician's Mate. He served aboard submarine tender USS *Canopus*, the submarine USS *Sealion*, and the Porpoise-class submarine USS *Perch* (SS 176).

It was during his assignment aboard *Perch* that he was captured by the Japanese.

While surfaced thirty miles northwest of Soerabaja, Java, March 1, 1942, *Perch* was attacked by Japanese destroyers. Driven down with a string of depth charges to a depth of 135 feet, and enduring several more depth charges, Turner and the men of *Perch* repaired the submarine and they were able to resurface early the next morning.

They were attacked again and again, and forced to submerge. Convinced that they had finished off the submarine by the oil loss and the air from damaged ballast tanks, the enemy left *Perch* and went hunting for other targets. That allowed *Perch* to again surface and conduct repairs.

On a dive to test those repairs, the submarine was forced to resurface and was engaged for what would be the final time by two enemy cruisers and three destroyers.

The commanding officer, Lt. Cmdr. David A. Hurt, ordered the ship to be abandoned and the submarine was scuttled.

In later years, Turner related the following passage concerning the event to friends Jeanine and Lorie Allen.

"As we were given the order to 'abandon the boat,' when *Perch* was going down, our captain, Lt. Cmdr. David Hurt, was the last man off the conning tower. We were in the water for a while before the Japanese came by to rescue our crew. We did not know if they were going to shoot us or abandon us to the sea. Hurt was having difficulty treading water as the Japanese ship was rescuing the crew using a rickety ladder."

The captain told Turner he "wasn't going to make it," and said, "Just leave me, Turk. I no longer have the strength to go on. Save yourself . . . leave me."

"I wasn't going to listen to that, so I dove down and came up right under him, and I pushed him right up the ladder with him still protesting," Turner told the Allens.

While the entire crew of sixty officers and enlisted sailors survived that day, six later died in Japanese POW camps. The survivors were later repatriated and were able to enjoy the victory over the Japanese in World War II from home.

After surviving cruel beatings, starvation, and tropical diseases at the POW camp on the island of Makassar Celebes, Turner came home October 17, 1945, and remained in the Navy until his retirement December 1, 1959.

Nearly seven decades after receiving his injuries while in captivity, Turner was presented the Purple Heart Medal on January 2, during a ceremony held at King's Grant Baptist Church in Virginia Beach. He was also awarded the Korean Service Medal for his service during that conflict.

Retired U.S. Navy Rear. Adm. Fred Metz awarded Turner the medals.

"If you think about what he had to endure, or anyone in the prisoner of war camps, a Purple Heart does not really signify what they had to go through," said Metz, "but it's one way this country honors the people who lived through those perils."

Turner was known by family and friends as a strong-willed veteran with an equally strong conviction for his country, but he always had a kind word for all. He was particularly fond of sharing his time and sea stories with fellow veterans.

"Turk showed us all courage and humility during and after facing the enormous struggle of a POW," said Captain Stephen T. Koehler, who pinned the medals on Turner and is currently commanding officer of amphibious assault ship USS *Bataan* (LHD 5). "He gave us perspective when we thought we were having a bad day. It only takes a thought of him with his struggle over sixty years ago, and the way he handled it with a positive attitude, to shed light on our current day-to-day problems."

"He became a friend and inspiration to both me and the crew of *Bataan* with this positive attitude and his zest for life," Koehler continued. "He spent a lot of his time with my young sailors telling stories and relating his time in submarines and as a POW, for which I am grateful. He was truly a great influence on *Bataan* sailors in our quest to keep *Bataan* Heritage part of our ship."

Ernest Plantz, one of Turner's shipmates on *Perch* and his cellmate while both were prisoners of war, personalized his convictions. "Turk was my mentor and best buddy," said Plantz, a friend of Turner's for sixty-nine years and the only surviving sailor from *Perch*. "He tutored me for my seaman qualifications and my submarine qualifications. He continued being an outstanding teacher throughout his life, relaying his experiences in the Navy. Turk loved people, with only good words for everyone. His deep faith saw him through many trials, and the love of his family helped him along the way. Turk will be remembered as one of the unsung heroes of his generation who served in the submarine force with honor and dignity. I loved you, shipmate, and treasured the friendship that we shared."

Ted Davis, a retired U.S. Navy captain and former commanding officer of the Tench-class diesel submarine USS *Grenadier* (SS-525), concurred with Plantz. "There is nothing Turk wouldn't do or has not already done for his country, his service, his friends, and his family," said Davis, a longtime friend and member of the Hampton Roads Chapter of the U.S. Submarine Veterans, Inc.

"Turk showed us the way a hero walks, softy with love in his heart. He may have spent many tours in Hell, but he served God and country for life."

Turner went on "eternal patrol" at the age of ninety-two, February 28, 2011.

He will be cremated and his remains scattered at sea during a future ceremony.

* * *

A tribute to Marion "Turk" Turner was published in *Polaris* magazine, June 2011. In it was mentioned that Marion "Turk" Turner was a member of the Submarine Veterans of WWII Tidewater Chapter, that he served as president, VP, and was a member of the Veterans of Foreign Wars (VFW), Fleet Reserve Associate (FRA), Holland Club, *Bataan Corregidor*, and was member of King Grant Baptist Church.

SAMUEL FORD SIMPSON (FORMER POW)

From a brief article on the USS *Perch* (formerly P-5) by Sam Simpson[3]

Having given all before me a chance to pay tribute to the gallant submarine USS *Perch* (formerly P-5), constructed at the E.B. Company in Groton, Connecticut, I hereby give my view on that great hunk of steel and of my shipmates that gave their all to keep her afloat.

---

[3] From the book *U.S. Submarine Veterans of World War II*, Volume Four (Taylor Publishing Company).

USS *Perch* (SS-176), photo courtesy of flickr.com via Bill Gonyo (NavSource)

"Pig Boats" they called them, but that name never applied to the USS *Perch*. She was the thriving home and pride of some fifty-five men. She was long and sleek and beautiful, with a bone in her mouth and as fancy as they come with her plume in full stream. She took her place, second to none. She steamed in the Atlantic, the Pacific, and the Indian oceans; from the Caribbean Sea to the Bering Sea; and from the Yellow Sea to the Java Sea. No doubt she passed the cracks in the ocean that Leviathan called his home many times.

Silent and seaworthy, she was a mighty fortress. Yet Portuguese man-of-wars sailed from her prow and flying fish flopped on her decks. When the seas were blue with a white fringe on top, a grateful crew sunned themselves on her topside. Some sailed kites, releasing handkerchief parachutes to fall into the sea. At other times there were turtle hunts and picnics and a swim call in the Sulu Sea. Yes, she was home away from home.

But there is another side to the *Perch*. After months at sea, she was gaunt and mossy, weathered by gales and typhoons. She prowled the seas looking for the enemy. She was the hunter on the trail of the hunted; the eyes of the front line, reporting the advance of the enemy. She was an artist at avoiding deception and cunning at deceiving the enemy.

A wisp of smoke, a glimpse of a mast behind a cloud, the silhouette of a possible target or the thud of a different propeller transformed her into something else—all eyes and ears to take her prey where she found it, making reports under way.

There were some disappointments and narrow escapes, like a circling torpedo, and a shell through the conning tower, scars from the raids on the enemy. Depth charge attacks were a common event in those days when the Rising Sun was still rising. Though the *Perch*'s hull was badly flattened and her hatches badly twisted, she leaked very little to the eye. She was strong. Though her propeller shaft was bent and her engines loose from their moorings, she held tight.

The acrid smoke from torpedoes that had run in their skids didn't help. It was the chlorine gas and steady buildup of water in several bilges that was to seal her fate. In the middle of the night, free from the bottom, she wallowed in the sea. No gauges, few lights. The getaway was slow.

Repairs having been completed, the predawn effort to submerge was made. The word came, "Take her down," but she wouldn't go! Like a giant dolphin she leaped and dove. Water poured under her twisted hatch covers, which would not seal. After several attempts to dive, and in the midst of the enemy shell fire, the word was passed to abandon ship. As I passed through the control room,

Charlie Cross, Chief of the Boat, on the manifold, said, "You had better hurry. She is settling in the water and could go at any time."

I sat on the deck aft taking off my shoes. She slipped from under me, and I floated off the deck into the sea and night.

Midst a background of red and yellow gun burst, she made a grand entry into the Java Sea. Going down by the stern, raising her prow to an angle of about 35, she gave her last salute and silently slipped backward into the sea. In retrospect, I recall several persons diving from the "A" frames into the sea just before she went down. All hands got off and we were later picked up by some of the Japanese fleet that had been shelling us. We were off-loaded several days later at Makassar, a city on the island of Celebes-Dutch East Indies. We were released from the Japanese on September 19, 1945, flown to Borneo, Philippines, Honolulu, San Francisco, Quantico, and Virginia.

The USS *Perch* and other submarines escorted the Fourth Marines out of Shanghai one week before the war started. The Marines were aboard the *Madison* and *Harrison*, old Dollar Line ships.

USS *Nautilus* (SF-9/SS-168)

USS *Nautilus* (SF-9/SS-168) was a *Narwhal*-class submarine and one of the "V-boats." She was commissioned on July 1, 1930. After completing her fourteenth, and last, patrol on January 30, 1945, she was finally decommissioned.

Information taken from https://en.wikipedia.org/wiki/ USS_Nautilus_(SS-168)

HANK KUDZIK, CPO CHIEF

From a C-SPAN presentation, American History TV C-SPAN, October 27, 2012[4]

My name is Hank Kudzik, and I come from Bethlehem, Pennsylvania. During World War II, I spent all my time on two submarines. I made fourteen war patrols, beginning with the Battle of Midway. We all know Midway was an air conflict. *So what was a submarine doing there?*

---

[4] http://www.c-span.org/video/?309083-5/battle-midway

December 7 changed my life completely. I was a sixteen-year-old kid who didn't know what to do with my life. So, after the Japanese bombed Pearl Harbor, two days after Christmas, in 1941, I went to the recruiting office. I didn't lie. I told them I was sixteen but I had a birthday coming up. I got a recruiter who listened to me, and he said, "We'll go through all the preliminaries and get you signed up, and all you have to do, son, is put up your hand and say, 'I do,'" or whatever it took. Finally, he said, "Son, you're in the Navy."

No mention of a submarine. I didn't even know what a submarine looked like. I couldn't tell the difference between a baby stroller and a submarine. I just wanted to go to war, but submarines were not in my plans. Things happened in the old days real quick. I didn't go to any school whatsoever. From boot camp, which was real quick, to the West Coast, I wound up in the Navy Yard at Pearl Harbor—and there were a lot of us. What did they do with us? They put us on work detail. My first work detail was helping to take the dead bodies off of the *Oklahoma* and the *Oglala*, not a very pleasant task. You're asking me to go back to 1942 and dig . . . and pick out all these things. Some of them . . . are very emotional for me . . .

I happened to be on a work detail on the carrier *Saratoga*, waiting to be assigned. I was in the freshwater tank, wire-brushing rust, when they decided to take her out on a shakedown. An explosion occurred. "What was that?" I asked "Get out of that tank!" someone said. So I got out of that tank. "What happened?" I asked again. "Oh, I don't know. Something put a hole in the water line," the other guy said. It was either a mine or a torpedo, but it was a hole, and we managed to get it back. When I crawled out of that freshwater tank, I didn't want any more part of aircraft carriers. I looked over and saw a submarine base, and I figured, well, maybe I ought to apply for something—I'd rather be on the end of shooting these torpedoes than receiving them.

I had to go to the chaplain, because the chief in charge of the work detail wouldn't let me go. The chaplain was very sympathetic. He said, "Son, do you know what you're getting into? I'll let you go over there and you can talk to them, and you bring me back a chit saying that they'll accept you. I'll free you from this work detail." That's exactly what happened. I wound up waiting to be assigned to a submarine.

Along came the submarine *Nautilus*, about the middle of May, and I became a crew member. This is what I wanted. I really wanted combat. I didn't want ship's company, anything like that. I wanted to get in there and sock it to them.

When we finally did get on our station, everybody was assigned to duty watch—four on, eight off, four on, eight off. This is what you do on a submarine. You don't eat three meals a day, because you are either sleeping or doing something else. It depends on what your hours are.

My watches were elbow-to-elbow with the XO, the skipper, and so forth. My watch was either in the control room, the conning tower, or the bridge. I wanted to get some fresh air! You never smelled such bad air in your life as you will on a submarine. If you can take that diesel smell—and you'll have caustic odors coming out of the batteries that disintegrate your clothes—if you can stand pressure and the foul air, maybe you can become a submariner.

There we sat on our patrol area, and a captain's dream—a flotilla of ships—came by . . . Did you know *Nautilus* was already twelve years old and a riveted submarine . . . Riveted?! What does that remind you of? The *Titanic* was riveted, and look what happened to her. We had a submarine with a half-inch pressure hull. Submarines have two hulls—a pressure hull and on the other side of that is the ballast hull. Between these two hulls was water.

The skipper said we were going to make ready (torpedo) tubes one, two, three, and four. *Here we go, we're going to shoot. Hallelujah, the first!* I was so excited, because this is what I wanted. I wanted to join the Navy and get into combat.

So the skipper fires. *Fire one! Fire two!* He didn't even have to turn the sub much . . . and then he fires two more—three and four. One hit, two hit, three hit—but no explosions. Disaster. We had fired four torpedoes. All of them hit, but we didn't sink a thing. But we paid for it! Now something else was new to us—depth charges. Boy, they came falling down, because they weren't going to let us get away. They pounded us with close to forty depth charges, which was the worst thing I ever heard in my life. Well, they had another mission—to get by us—and they didn't spend too much time on that, so we managed to survive their attack.

The next day and a half, a strange thing happened. Every so often when you're submerged, you take a look around, because you don't want any surprises to surface. I spotted some smoke on the horizon . . . I talked to the XO. "I see smoke." He said, "Okay, let me take a look. You're right, Hank. There is smoke there. Let's investigate." Well, we get up on the surface and we start to head toward the smoke. Guess what it was? An aircraft carrier. Hallelujah! Now it couldn't happen again—we couldn't shoot more torpedoes and have them not go off. "C'mon," I insisted. "Okay, we'll track this guy," the XO said. His friend, and my captain, Bill Brockman, said we would get as close as we could. In submarine fights you want to fire torpedoes at 1,500 yards or less, not greater than that. You want to be between the 1,000 yard mark and the 1,500 mark. How about 700 yards? That's how close we were. The captain could read some of the Japanese insignias on the *Soryu*. That's how close we were.

"Make tubes ready, one, two, and three," he ordered. Okay, they were ready to go; now you fire from the conning tower. "Fire one, fire two, fire three!" Number one hit, number two hit, number three hit. Water has a very good acoustical sound. You could hear everything. One exploded, two exploded, three did not. We had problems at the beginning of the war with torpedoes not exploding, but here we got two fish that were enough to take the *Soryu* to a tremendous list. They were patching her up, because they wanted to land some planes and their carriers were sunk. Those planes were either going to land in the water or land on a hard surface, and the *Soryu* was that. But we sank the *Soryu*; we sank the carrier. We got so close we could spit at the destroyer, and we sank her with one torpedo. And now there was another destroyer. The next day she came after us, because she was determined to get the *Nautilus*.

My XO was a camera nut, and he wanted to find a way to take a picture through the periscope. The skipper was happier than hell. He said, "Ozzie, Ozzie, did you see it? Did you see it?" Ozzie had used a device. He said, "I didn't see a thing, Captain." Of course he didn't, the camera saw it. When he looked, there was nothing there. But when he developed the picture, this is what he got." [He shows a picture from a 1942 magazine.] "This was the first picture taken of an American submarine sinking an enemy vessel. In the U.S.A., you know, they wanted to know how the war was going . . .

* * *

Henry "Hank" Kudzik CPO served from 1942 to 1944 on the USS *Nautilus* (SS-168) and six war patrols on the USS *Gar* (SS-206). Awards include Navy and Marine Commendation Medal, Navy Presidential Unit Citation, World War II Victory Medal, Philippine Presidential Unit Citation, and Philippine Liberation.

USS *Nautilus* (SS-168); photo courtesy of Henry "Hank" Kudzik

JEROME S. GROSS
"*Nautilus* & Battle at Midway"
Written by Jerome S. Gross
Reprinted from *Polaris* / March 2012

The astounding success of the Pearl Harbor assault by Japanese aircraft on Black Sunday, December 7, 1941, left our Navy mortally wounded. Our capital ships, the pride of our naval fleet, lay decimated—burning hulks floundering in the mud of Battleship Row. Members of the Japanese high command, exalting over their triumphant victory, assumed their armada now had the license to roam carte blanche throughout the vast Pacific sea-lanes. As history has proven, the greatest miscalculation suffered by the Japanese imperial command was to consistently depreciate the potential effectiveness of America's submarine fleet.

Clandestine intelligence reports revealed an attack on our base at Midway Island was imminent. Preparing for the anticipated battle, our submarine, the USS *Nautilus*, was assigned to an area northwest of the atoll.

On the morning of June 1, 1942, masts appearing below the horizon proved to be an enemy task force. According to our calculations, a battleship protected by a screen of escorting cruisers was on course leading directly to our sector. We manned our battle stations submerged—the first time in actual wartime conditions.

Our torpedo attack on the battleship was thwarted when one of the cruisers, alerted by the plumb of our protruding periscope, came charging toward us at high speed. We were forced deep to evade the impending onslaught.

On the way down, several patterns of terrifying, earsplitting explosions shattered our virginity. Their ungodly detonations, reverberating through the hull, sounded and felt nothing like the insignificant pops of exploding hand grenades used in our indoctrination.

Returning to periscope depth (quoting our Captain Brockman's patrol report), "Ships were on all sides of us, moving at high speed. Our target, the battleship, lay on our port side firing her whole starboard broadside at us." With the proper trajectory determined by our Torpedo Data Computer, we fired, but our torpedoes missed.

Utilizing the wakes of our expended torpedoes as a directional guide, the enemy bore down on us like a swarm of wasps. Their carefully coordinated counterattack was unmercifully executed. We were bombed and strafed repeatedly by aircraft, and we came perilously close to being rammed and depth charged with a vengeance by the escorts. We flooded negative (tank) and rapidly descended to a safe depth.

Far below the surface, there was ample time to reflect on a nerve-shattering experience none of us onboard could have imagined. It was truly our Baptism of Fire.

Later in the day, smoke on the horizon revealed a slow moving, apparently damaged aircraft carrier escorted by two cruisers. We manned our battle stations and fired a salvo of three torpedoes from the forward tubes. We were committed, our hearts beating wildly as the seconds ticked on. With his eye glued to the periscope, the captain continuously tracked the torpedo wakes running straight and true toward the target.

Suddenly from the conning tower came this exuberant shout, "A HIT!—TWO!—THREE!" Once again quoting from the patrol report, "Red flames appearing along the length of the ship from the bow to amidships."

To evade the imminent counterattack by rapidly approaching cruisers, we took her down to a comparatively safe depth.

After surfacing we observed our victim—the abandoned Japanese aircraft carrier *Soryu*, now a fiercely burning hulk—begin her slow descent beneath the sea. She had the distinction of being the first enemy vessel sunk by torpedoes fired by the *Nautilus* during World War II.

Our "rite of passage" was confirmed by President Roosevelt and Secretary of State Knox by their presentation of the Presidential Unit Citation presented to the *Nautilus* for scoring the fatal blow against an aircraft carrier of 10,000 tons in the battle of Midway.

When the hostilities had subsided, we were directed to put in at the submarine facility at Midway to refuel and replenish our expended torpedoes.

Our brief stay at Midway provided us with the luxury of a freshwater shower. With the island enclosed in a complete blackout, the bright moonlight prescribed a line in the reflecting sand around bomb blasted craters to the shower room.

Later that evening, some of us met with a group of unwinding Marines in their underground bunkers. In the confines of that hot, humid, sweat-laden cubicle, we discussed the exciting events that had transpired that day. Little did we know at the time that today's battle would represent the decisive turning point in our war with Japan.

The next day we departed Midway en route to our newly assigned patrol area off the coast of Honshu. There we attacked and photographed the sinking Japanese destroyer, *Yamakaze*, reputed to be the first successful picture taken through a submarine periscope. It was featured on the cover of *Life* magazine as the "Picture of the Week."

BOOTS HANSON

"Gun Running *Nautilus*"

Written by Boots Hanson

Reprinted from *Polaris* / June 2014

The ability to think clearly in dangerous situations and the importance of teamwork are the sorts of lessons learned while serving in submarines. I was one of those men, a sign painter apprentice, who enlisted in the Navy in 1943. I volunteered for submarine duty and went to Pearl Harbor, undergoing training and working in a relief crew.

I joined the crew of the *Nautilus* (SS-168) in April 1944. It was built in the 1920s and was one of the largest subs the U.S. Navy ever built. She had two six-inch deck guns and extra torpedoes under her raised gun deck. She already had a good war record, sending enemy ships to the bottom, including a Japanese destroyer. She also participated in the Battle of Midway.

With her spacious interior, she could carry soldiers for raids on remote islands in the Pacific. On my eighteenth birthday, we departed Australia for my first war patrol. Within two days we had to dive from an attacking allied aircraft.

We were laden with volatile munitions, drums of gasoline, and important passengers. *Nautilus* did her best to avoid numerous Japanese patrol boats and aircraft. Bombs were dropped and depth charges came close, but the missions were always completed successfully. Because the extra torpedoes were removed to make room for cargo, the boat's offensive capabilities were limited, but the skipper did take time to blow a pair of enemy supply ships out of the water with her deck guns.

The most dangerous part of the mission was the off-loading of cargo. Surfacing at night, the sub would come as close to shore as possible, always in water too shallow in which to submerge. Working in total darkness, the weapons, food, and medical supplies would be passed up through the hatches and handed down to Filipinos gathered around in small boats.

Near the island of Cebu, *Nautilus* ran aground. With dawn would come patrol planes, and the sub would surely be spotted. Everything possible was removed from the vessel and put over the side to lighten the boat. Flood ballasts were blown dry and trim tanks were emptied, but still nothing seemed to help in getting the boat off the reef.

With only an hour before dawn, secret papers were burned and explosive charges were set to blow up the boat. It seemed the crew was destined to become guerilla fighters. Finally, as the tide went out, more fuel was pumped over the side, and a final effort was made to get the sub free. With engines roaring at full throttle in reverse, the sub began to slide off the shoal. Since most of the crew had abandoned ship, they were taken back on board as soon as the depth of water was sufficient to handle the weight.

Nautilus made an untrimmed emergency dive to evade any spying eye. She continued running guns to the Philippines until ordered home in early 1945, after fourteen war patrols. Being an apprentice painter, I assisted in painting the enemy ships sunk on the side of the sub's sail.

Returning home to Houston, Texas, as a machinist mate, I took on the job of oil well firefighting. With all the skills of my learning in a submarine, I could calmly face raging infernos and win the battles.

USS *Scorpion* (SS-278)

USS *Scorpion* (SS-278) was a *Gato*-class submarine. She was commissioned on October 1, 1942. On January 5, 1944, she sent her final communication about a crew member who had fractured his foot when he dropped a crate of oranges on it. She was not seen or heard from again.

Information taken from https://en.wikipedia.org/wiki/USS _Scorpion_(SS-278)

GAIL L. DIAMOND

Information submitted by Gail L. Diamond to Mary Nida Smith

The USS *Scorpion* was commissioned at Portsmouth, New Hampshire, in October 1942. The commanding officer was Lt. Cmdr. William N. Wylie, and the executive officer was Lt. Cmdr. R. M. Raymond. The executive officer's job aboard ship was to get all the experience required before getting his own command.

The crew consisted of nine officers and sixty enlisted men. Rigorous training prepared them for any emergencies that would happen. The training continued as the boat sailed to Panama, traveling through the canal and on to Pearl Harbor. One of the crew members was First Class Torpedoman Gail L. Diamond, in charge of the after torpedo room. Here is his story:

On April 5, 1943, the boat left Pearl Harbor for its first war patrol. In the forward torpedo room it carried eleven torpedoes and twelve mines. The after room had three torpedoes and ten mines. Diamond's main priority was to lay twenty-two mines in the traffic lanes inside Yokohama Harbor, which was on the main Japanese Island of Honshu.

"After we had laid the mines, we were free to use the ship's guns and torpedoes to attack the Japanese.

"We crossed the International Date Line on April 10, and that day was lost according to the calendar. We were making about fifteen knots per hour. About 0200 on the morning of April 19, we approached the Japanese coast and the lookouts began sighting Japanese boats. At one time eight small vessels were in view. Some were patrol boats and others were fishermen.

"Most of the little boats were from thirty to sixty feet long. No guns were visible on them," said Diamond. "Executive Officer Raymond made the remark, 'We could hold a field day on these little boats before we leave to go back to Pearl Harbor.'"

The crew members' first concern was to lay their mines.

"At about 2100 hours, we heard a terrible banging sound on the outside of the boat that startled us all. Most of us were scared. Not even the captain knew what was happening.

"Later, we determined the submarine was hung up in a Japanese fishing net. The crashing noise was the glass balls attached to the net banging against the hull. When the balls had broken, the banging ceased. Most of the net clung to the boat until we surfaced," Diamond said. "There was lots of confusion and noise. Immediately the patrol boats were alerted. Two of them tried to locate us with grappling hooks. The clanging of the chains on deck rattled the full length of the submarine. This added more fear to all of us."

In an attempt to escape the patrol boats, they made a quick dive and leveled off at 430 feet. "The boat had been tested for only 300 feet. We feared the hull and seam would not hold up to that depth, but they did," said Diamond with a sigh, as if he was reliving it all over again.

When the sound above them stopped and everything appeared to be cleared, they worked their way close to the beach and prepared to lay mines. The mines were slightly less than twenty-one inches in diameter. Two mines were stored on one torpedo skid, and they fit snugly into the torpedo tubes when they were ready to fire.

One at a time, the mines were shot out of the torpedo tubes with compressed air, same as a torpedo. Sea water rushed into the open torpedo tube after the firing. The air used to push out the mines was bled back into the submarine to prevent a bubble rising to the surface. The extra air increased the pressure in the boat. They could not run the air compressors because of the noise they would make.

Each mine was equipped with calibrated control equipment, including a time clock and depth regular. The regulars were set before they could fire. There was no propulsion unit on the mines, so they would sink to the bottom shortly after leaving the torpedo tube.

The crew in the forward room started laying mines at about 1700 hours. The twelve mines were out and the job completed in about an hour and a quarter. At 1830 hours, the after room started laying ten mines.

"The mines we had laid were resting on the bottom at the depth of about 200 feet. Our escape route was back over them," said Diamond. "The clocks on the mines were set to start releasing a cable with the explosive head in about three hours. A cable arrangement allowed the buoyant explosive head to slowly rise in the water to their assigned depth—about ten feet. The charge would be ignited by contact with a ship.

"At 2015 we surfaced, after being submerged sixteen hours and fifteen minutes. Everyone was complaining of headaches because of the pressure inside the boat. The increase in pressure made most of us very uncomfortable," said Diamond, "and it was darn hot."

At about 1130 hours on Tuesday, April 20, the alarm sounded for them to go to their battle stations.

"The executive officer passed the word over the loudspeakers that a freighter was in view about 7,000 yards away, and it appeared to be the enemy. The order was given to have three torpedoes ready in the forward torpedo room. Roughly four minutes later, the after torpedo room was given the instructions. Immediately, the order was given: *Stand by to fire aft. Fire 8, Fire 9, Fire 7.*"

"What seemed a very long time was actually only a few minutes, before we heard the explosion of the torpedoes. We knew then that we had made the kill. Through the periscope, the captain could see eight survivors clinging to three different pieces of wreckage.

"It was real exciting for me. I had painted *Norma*, my wife's name at that time, on the torpedo that hit the ship. Everyone in the after torpedo room were all hyped up with excitement of our first hit. The *Scorpion* wasn't a virgin anymore."

Minutes after midnight on April 21, they dove and prepared for their battle stations—deck guns. As the gun crew waited in the conning tower, the captain told them they had a boat lined up to sink. It was about 160 feet long with a twenty-foot beam. There was no way to determine whether she was armed. But they were ordered to try their luck with using the deck guns.

The three-inch gun crew included the trainer, sight setter, first loader, hot shell man, second loader, and several ammunition passers. Diamond's battle station was a trainer. His responsibility was to move the gun horizontally. Mack was the pointer who moved the gun with a foot lever when given the word by the sight setter.

"I was a wee bit scared, as many of us were. The gun crew had fired the three-inch gun many times in practice. This was the first time at a live target. We had never been in a position where someone might shoot back at us," said Diamond.

"We surfaced at 0050 and manned all guns. In addition to the three-inch, we had two 20-mms, a couple of 30-cals, and two Tommy guns. The first shell we fired in the three-inch was a misfire. Wrong time for that to happen," remarked Diamond. "The target was 1,000 yards away, and we were headed straight for it."

They continued to move forward toward the target, with the 20-mm gunner firing like hell. When their gun was clear and reloaded, Mack and Diamond trained on the target while the sight setter gave the word to fire. The first went through the wheelhouse. The second hit below the deck and ripped a big hole. The 20-mms were raking the target vessel from bow to stern. The next three-inch shell hit the enemy's engine, causing it to explode, and fire broke out on mid-ship.

"Suddenly our soundman picked up the noise of a set of screws—an enemy's boat propeller. We wasted no time in getting out of there," said Diamond.

"At 2330 the lookouts sighted another patrol boat, and they were called back to man the 20-mm and 30-cal. guns. The three-inch gun crew waited impatiently to be called to action. When the sub had made the approach, at 600 yards from the patrol boat, the gun crew opened fire. In one minute and thirty-five seconds, the boat, about the size as the last one, was sinking stern first.

"Our action was not unnoticed by the enemy. Four hours after we had attacked the vessel, around 0400, a plane was picked up on the SD radar coming in FAST! About that same time a tin can, a destroyer, suddenly appeared, coming in after us at about thirty-five knots. We crash-dived to 380 feet.

"We heard a couple of depth charges in the distance. It didn't shake us. A second destroyer came." The two searched for them until about noon that day.

"Friday, April 23, started off with a hell of a bang. At 0010 another patrol boat was sighted. Again the 20-mm and the 30-cal. gun crews were called to their battle stations. The crew opened up on the target at about 650 yards. There were lights on the boat, and after the first gunshot blast they were out. In a minute and forty-five seconds, the boat was gone. She weighed about fifty tons. While our gun crew was still on deck, another patrol boat was sighted. We went after it. In what seemed like only two minutes, that boat was history. There were no survivors on any of the three boats."

Diamond had just been called for the 0400 watch when word was passed that they had a target of about 15,000 tons in sight. It was escorted by two destroyers. In a few more minutes, another ship was sighted. "At about 0415 the forward torpedo room was instructed to make all ready. We fired four torpedoes at the big ship and one at a smaller vessel. About a minute later we heard a loud explosion, followed by others. Quickly we dove 380 feet and underwent a depth charge attack. We went deeper to 440 feet. That was the deepest the boat had ever dived. The crew was afraid the captain would take them deeper.

"When the depth charges stopped, we rose to periscope depth to check on the damage we had effected with our torpedoes. One of the ships was in flames and her speed was slackened to five knots.

"On April 27, we dove at 0330 as daylight approached. An hour later the word was passed that a convoy was approaching. Four merchant ships escorted one destroyer. Our boat started the approach when the convoy was about 2,500 yards away. All six torpedo tubes in the forward room were prepared to fire. When the convoy came within 2,200 yards of our boat, we fired four torpedoes at the largest ship—a 9,000-ton vessel. The first explosion came within a minute and a half, and the second one followed about ten seconds later. Two more torpedoes were fired at the second ship, quickly followed by more torpedoes.

"The huge destroyer escort was heading toward us at high speed. There was no longer time to see if the first ship was sinking. We instantly dove to 250 feet! In my opinion, it wasn't deep enough. Suddenly all hell broke loose," Diamond said.

"Eight 600-pound depth charges were dropped on us. So far, we had received no damage. When it appeared quiet and no more depth charges would be coming, we surfaced. The freighter had its bow sticking straight up. The captain took some pictures before the Japanese ship made its final plunge to the bottom. We had to be careful. The enemy was still patrolling the area. A Japanese plane spotted us. We dove to 200 feet. We were lucky—no damage. Through our hull we could hear the target ship breaking up as it was engulfed by the sea."

The morning of April 28, at 0600, *Scorpion* cruised on the surface with the periscope watch on duty. The man at the periscope spotted an enemy patrol boat. The captain ordered all 20-mm and 30-cal. crews topside.

"At about 1,800 yards, the gun crews shot the hell out of it, but the boat would not sink! Our captain quickly called up the three-inch gun crew."

Mack and Diamond took up their positions. They fired twenty rounds and got eighteen hits. They were within 1,000 yards of the enemy boat. It was pitching as the wheelhouse was blown away. Three crew members were clinging to the stern of the boat. It was burning intensely.

The gunnery officer wanted Mack and Diamond to get more practice. They continued to fire nineteen more times until there was nothing left of the boat.

"April 30, a Friday, I remember it as if it was yesterday. It was the saddest day, one that would be ingrained in my mind the rest of my life," Diamond said.

"We had returned to the battle at a range of 1,500 yards. We missed with the first three-inch shot. The second hit the bridge, causing a fire, followed by ten rounds laid along her water line. As we moved in closer, we discovered it wasn't the target we thought it was. It wasn't a man-of-war, an enemy boat with guns.

"The crew on the enemy patrol boat had a three-inch gun forward and another aft. We fired at them with machine guns and high-powered rifles. *Scorpion's* small arms crew had the range. The lead was hitting the enemy's conning tower with a THUD. Every hit made a hole in their superstructure. Our gunners had not found the range with their three-inch guns. We were getting close, for we could hear the projectiles hit the water.

"I trained on the target's forward three-inch gun. I made three direct hits. Then we shifted to focus on their after gun. We knocked it out with four shots. Suddenly the captain shouted, "They've killed Mr. Raymond!"

"It's like being hit yourself by the enemy's gun, and you want to take revenge one more time. For a few minutes more, we furiously opened up on the vessel with all our guns. The captain ordered us to secure the three-inch gun. He then ordered the forward torpedo room to prepare the one remaining torpedo ready to fire. As it fired the captain said, '*This* is for Mr. Raymond.'"

Their last fish hit the vessel squarely. It was the largest explosion Diamond had ever witnessed in this life. One section of the ship sank in about thirty seconds. The excitement level on deck was high. The three-inch gun crew was ordered below. Suddenly *Scorpion's* radar picked up a plane bearing down on them at a distance of two miles.

"We made a crash dive. There was no time to bring Mr. Raymond below. He was lost in the foaming sea," said Diamond. "The plane dropped one bomb, but it didn't touch us."

When they were safely under the water, the crew had time to assess the damage. Five were hit by small arms fire. The gun boss was hit in the zipper of his sub jacket. The metal zipper had deflected the bullet, and he received only a break in his skin.

Diamond took a hit in his leg, but not a direct hit. The bullet had ricocheted off the gun mount. Three other men on the gun crew, including the loader, had been hit.

Diamond said, "This is one memory I'll carry with me the rest of my life." They had lost one of the most respected men aboard their submarine. Executive Officer R. M. Raymond was lost because of a 600-ton armed, 225-foot-long enemy patrol boat.

"We headed the USS *Scorpion* to Pearl Harbor for repairs, supplies, and a little R&R. The commanding officer of the Pacific Fleet sent us a message with a Letter of Commendation on the success of our first war patrol. In the letter it said all the ships in the U.S. forces should look up to us because of our valiant work. Medals were awarded for bravery during that action. The first class gunner's mate received a Silver Star for his action in clearing the misfire. Five of the crew received the Purple Heart."

* * *

Scorpion was reported to be presumed lost on March 6, 1944, while on her fourth war patrol. All the shipmates continue on "Eternal Patrol." Diamond had left *Scorpion* because of a leg wound and had been shipped back to the States to help train the crew for another submarine.

Other submarines Diamond sailed on were the *Pike* (SS-173), *Tullibee* (SS-284), *Tilefish* (SS-307), *Catfish* (SS-339), *Bashaw* (SS-241), and the *Rongull* (SS-396).

Gail L. Diamond TMC (SS) was born in Mankato, Kansas. He joined the Navy in 1939 and retired in 1966 after serving twenty-six years in the Navy. He lived in Idaho where he was a member of the Holland Club, an award given to all U.S. Submarine Veterans who have qualified in submarines for fifty years or longer and are in good standing in the United States Submarine Veterans, Inc. He rested his oars December 29, 2005, at Twin Falls, Idaho, and is now on "Eternal Patrol." He and his wife Dorothy Hanes Diamond had been married thirty-four years. Gail was ninety years old.

USS *Sawfish* (SS-276)

> **USS *Sawfish* (SS-276)** was a *Gato*-class submarine. She was commissioned on August 26, 1942. On March 10, 1945, she sailed her tenth, and last, war patrol. She received eight battle stars for her World War II service.
>
> *Information taken from https://en.wikipedia.org/wiki/USS _Sawfish_(SS-276)*

JAMES E. SCOTT, CPHM
Written by Lois Scott
Reprinted from *Polaris* / February 2007

This story is written by Lois Scott to share the stories her husband (nickname "Doc") had wanted to share, though he departed on his last patrol on August 15, 2006. His three children wished he had written about some of his most dangerous war patrols on the three submarines that he spent aboard through 1942–1945.

The USS *Sawfish* (SS-276), with Lt. Commander Eugene T. Sands, USN in command, sailed from Pearl Harbor in January

1943 to head for waters off southwestern Japan. She battle-surfaced to destroy a small patrol vessel with gunfire, then stalked a freighter that proved to be Russian. Later the same day, she had torpedo hits on a large freighter and the escorts were exploding depth charges all around, but she escaped unharmed.

Sawfish sighted five ships guarded by a destroyer, and as she headed for the largest freighter, it zigged toward her. The captain got a "down-the-throat" shot, which sank her. *Sawfish* evaded the depth charges.

Many years later, Jim enjoyed reading about some of the patrols of the *Sawfish*. He said it was funny how you remembered things. He thought they had the hell beat out of them many times, but that was not indicated in the reports.

The *Sawfish* and the *Wahoo* (SS-238) left Pearl to patrol in the Sea of Japan. They headed for passage through La Perouse Straits and they were aided by heavy rain, rough seas, and low visibility. Inside the Japanese Sea, a small coastal freighter was sighted. Torpedoes did not detonate. The target gave no evidence of any knowledge it had been fired upon. A heavy thump was heard and thereafter not heard to run. They believed the torpedo sank upon clearing the tube.

This was a most disappointing attack. The torpedoes did not explode at the end of the run. They began checking everything and it was concluded that the torpedoes were duds. At this point, there had been no contact with the *Wahoo*.

They saw no evidence of mines in the Straits or the Sea of Japan, but a plane was sighted. *Sawfish* dove and the plane dropped one bomb, so they were caught. They began to make their way slowly underwater to the Straits with several planes searching the vicinity, dropping bombs continuously. They evaded a patrol boat that had been sending depth charges. The patrol was terminated by their decision to carry remaining torpedoes back to base for examination as a result of faulty performance.

They were depth charged for hours, but the *Sawfish* needed to recharge batteries, which has to be done surfaced. The men were panting, but they were almost to the Straits. Captain Sands told Jim to get rid of his Masonic ring, in case they were taken prisoner, as the Japanese were known to torture them if they saw the Masonic emblem.

It was dark and they were again lucky with heavy rain, so they managed to get out and surface so they could run faster and also recharge their batteries. Back at Pearl they heard that the USS *Wahoo* was lost.

On another patrol, they spotted a large ship with two destroyer escorts. Captain Sands was a good shot, and a couple of torpedoes headed for the ship. Suddenly, the captain noticed the two destroyers were running away from the ship as fast as they could. *Sawfish* surfaced quickly. It was an ammunition ship, and the successful torpedo attack resulted in the largest explosion Jim had ever heard. It stopped the *Sawfish* dead in the water. The captain was a quick thinking skipper, or they might have been lost.

Jim told about a time they used grappling hooks in Tokyo Bay as they were trying to get away from two patrol boats that were combing the area.

He also loved to tell about the time they were on the surface when the sun was shining and it was a beautiful morning. The captain motioned for him to come to forward deck and said, "You've got to see this." There were several flying fish leaping out of the ocean, and the sun was like a spotlight on them. All of a sudden a giant fish jumped out of the water, his tail twisting and turning, and it caught a flying fish in midair. Jim said it took his breath away. That picture would stay with him forever.

There was humor on the boat. Jim and another crew member named Smart decided to create a newsletter once a week with jokes on the guys, and they put an ad in it called "The Smart-Smart-Scott Laundry Service." Then the next week it was "The Scott-Scott-Smart Laundry Service."

The next submarine he was assigned to was the USS *Besugo* (SS-321). While patrolling they surfaced, and a small boat could see their silhouette by the moon and started shooting at them. They used their deck gun and there was quite a battle. All of a sudden the *Besugo*'s gun jammed. The patrol boat machine gunned them and struck a lookout in the leg and the gunnery officer in the hand. Jim was busy doctoring.

Jim also had trouble with one young guy who was accident-prone. He was tall and slender and couldn't go through the door without hitting his head, so Jim would patch him up. Time and again he would get hurt, or when they stopped at a small island he drank the local gilly and he would get sick. Jim had to clean him up, and he finally told him never come to him again if he got into trouble. One day they were on deck, and there was an accident with the deck gun. You guessed it . . . it caught him on the head and almost killed him. As they were carrying him away he just kept repeating, "Don't tell the Doc!"

Toward the last of the war, Jim was chief of the boat on the USS *Hardhead* (SS-365). They were in the China Sea heading for Pearl and were out of coffee and other supplies, when they met the USS *Bullhead* going out on patrol. They begged for coffee and the *Bullhead* replied that they needed all their supplies, but they did exchange movies. The *Hardhead* had to go on their way. Later, the crew on the *Hardhead* heard a big explosion, and afterward they found out it was the *Bullhead*. [The *Bullhead* was the last submarine lost in the war.]

The *Hardhead* was patrolling in that same area, but it was just not their time.

Now, perhaps Jim is meeting some of his old buddies up there and they are reliving the stories of World War II.

* * *

USS BESUGO (SS-321) mascot "Sugi."

Mascot Sugi on USS *Besugo* (SS-321), photo courtesy of Submarine Vetarans of WWII

Polaris editor William R. Wolfe added a footnote at the end of this story: "Although not mentioned in the story, 'Sugi,' the seagoing mutt, was an integral part of the *Besugo*'s ships company."

USS *S-28* (SS-133)

USS *S-28* (SS-133) was an S-class submarine of the United States Navy, commissioned on December 13, 1923. A diesel submarine, she served during World War II, during which she accounted for the sinking of one Japanese ship. Later, during an exercise, she was lost at sea along with her entire crew.

Information taken from https://en.wikipedia.org/wiki/USS _S-28_(SS-133)

MELVIN TOLBERT SMITH, STC (SS) USN (RET)

"Close Encounter Remembering *S-28*"

As told to Mary Nida Smith

Reprinted from *Polaris* / October 2006

In June 1943, I went to boot camp at Farragut, Idaho, for six weeks. Then I had a week's leave before heading to Mare Island for a couple of weeks before going on to Pearl Harbor. I was seventeen years old and a seaman first class. I was assigned on September 20, 1943, to Subdivision 22 Relief Crew, and later reassigned as Submarine Division 45 Flag and Relief Crew, where I worked in the office doing odd jobs.

Sometime between September 20 and December 11, 1943, the office yeoman assigned me two weeks, training duty on the *S-28*, where I was involved in sonar/sound exercises to become a radioman striker. I had just finished my first week and was going into my second week. When I arrived to go aboard, my jaw was swollen from a bad tooth. The chief told me to go and take care of it on the USS *Holland*.

The next morning, I went down to finish my second week's training, but I couldn't find the *S-28*. So, I went back to the office where I worked and asked, "Where is the *S-28*? I can't find it." The yeoman answered, "Don't you ever ask that question again! Go back to work." Being from the "Silent Service," I learned early on to keep my mouth shut. I never heard a word from anyone—no chatter or newspaper reports. I didn't know what had happened. I was puzzled as I continued working on Relief Crew.

I was later assigned to the USS *Snapper* (SS-185), where I did three war patrol runs: the ninth, tenth, and eleventh. When we returned to the States at Mare Island Navy Shipyard for overhaul, I learned the *S-28* had sunk. All sailors were lost. It was the first time I had heard anything. I assumed it had happened when I was taking classes, the time I couldn't find it and the yeoman had told me never to ask questions again.

All these years I have carried some guilt regarding why I was saved and not aboard, and many questions still fill my mind: *Where did it go? Why was I told not to speak of it?* I never heard what happened until nine months later, after I returned from three patrols.

The story I heard was that they were training on a target, an old four-piper destroyer, when *S-28* dove and never came up. No signal, no nothing. When I was training on it, it never went below ninety feet and it leaked like a sieve. Near Pearl Harbor, outside the channel, is the second deepest spot in the world, four miles deep. Did it go down here or where? So much I didn't understand. It is an ongoing mystery—the lost *S-28* and its crew of forty-nine men.

I received my second *Y. D. Dandy-Gram* about the memorial being built. [*The Y. D. Dandy-Gram* was a newsletter published by North Carolina Submarine Veterans in memory of crew members of the USS *S-28* who gave their lives during World War II.] It all came bouncing back down on top of me after my wife decided to download information on the *S-28*. The headlines read: "Commander Submarine Force, U.S. Pacific Fleet USS *S-28* (SS-133) July 4, 1944—49 Men Lost." Here I had thought it went down in 1943, when it came up missing for my second week class.

Sixty-three years is a long time to ponder over the first Navy sea accident in the life of a young boy.

USS *Seal* (SS-183)

USS *Seal* (SS-183) was a *Salmon*-class submarine. She was commissioned on April 30, 1937. The USS *Seal* (SS-183) was awarded ten battle stars for her service during World War II.

Information taken from https://en.wikipedia.org/wiki/ USS_Seal_(SS-183)

JOSEPH T. BLANCHETT

Information submitted by Joseph T. Blanchett to Mary Nida Smith

Joseph T. Blanchett was born August 22, 1922, in southwest Kansas. In the spring of 1942, he graduated from high school, and on September 10, 1942, he joined the Navy. While in boot camp he volunteered for submarine service, and then he attended submarine school at New London, Connecticut, where he was trained in all aspects of operating a submarine. After graduating in May 1943, he was sent to Pearl Harbor Submarine Base, where he served with a relief crew for three months while waiting to be assigned to a boat and sea duty.

The relief crew's job is to prepare a submarine commissioned for sea duty or to refit submarines that arrive for shore duty while the regular crew is on R&R. They would clean, paint, and do repairs. Every job prepared the young seaman for his assigned sea duty aboard a boat that would be his home for several months at sea.

Joe Blanchett was assigned to the USS *Seal* (SS-183) in August 1943, when it sailed on its eighth war patrol. This was his *first* war patrol. On August 31, while making a routine dive, the conning tower hatch failed to latch—allowing water to rapidly fill the pump room, where it damaged the electrical circuits. Panic set in as they promptly brought the boat topside.

"This, my first patrol, was almost my last. It was very harrowing, needless to say," remarked Blanchett as he recalled how they moved slowly east, making temporary repairs that continued for a week.

On September 8, the air compressors were rigged to provide enough air pressure so that torpedoes could be launched when needed. They continued to the Kurels and crossed into the Sea of Okhotsk to continue their war patrol. On October 4, 1943, they returned to Pearl Harbor for refit after fifty days at sea.

"While at Pearl, I remember the Black Cat Café in Honolulu, Hawaii, where the special on Friday was cold pig's feet served with potato salad for twenty cents. The Royal Hawaii Hotel is what most sailors remember. Not me. I remember the pig's feet, for they were so good."

On the ninth and tenth patrol they were assigned to conduct photographic reconnaissance of Japanese bases in the Marshall Islands. "I think a lot of this information has not been released," said Blanchett. "Many of us ex-submarine sailors feel we didn't do anything adventurous. We were just doing our job and trying to survive."

With several other U.S. submarines, the USS *Seal* crew provided lifeguard services and conducted photographic reconnaissance, photographing enemy bases, defenses, installations, and beaches before they proceeded to Midway for overhaul.

Seal's twelfth and final war patrol lasted about thirty days at sea before they arrived at Pearl Harbor. "She was retired to training service both at Pearl and also after we returned to New London, Connecticut. I was transferred from the *Seal* to the New London Submarine Base until I was discharged on December 20, 1945," stated Blanchett.

* * *

At the time of this writing, Joseph T. Blanchett was a charter member of the U.S. Submarines Veterans of World War II, where he had been active for over fifty-two years. He and his lovely wife, Twila, lived in Newport, Arkansas.

USS *Billfish* (SS-286)

USS ***Billfish*** **(SS-286)** was a *Balao*-class submarine. She was commissioned on April 20, 1943. Between August 12, 1943, and August 27, 1945, *Billfish* made eight war patrols out of Pearl Harbor. During these patrols she sank three freighters totaling 4,074 tons and five smaller craft. She received seven battle stars for her World War II service.

Information taken from https://en.wikipedia.org/wiki/USS _Billfish_(SS-286)

JOHN D. RENDERNICK

Written by Captain James Bloom (Ret)

This article is reprinted with permission by Captain James Bloom, MC, USN (Ret)

TODAY IN NAVAL HISTORY, NOVEMBER 11–12, 1943—ATTACK ON *BILLFISH*

Late this afternoon, USS *Billfish* (SS-286) rested at periscope depth in Makassar Strait when overhead, a Japanese spotter plane recognized her submerged silhouette. The plane vectored a nearby destroyer and dropped a smoke marker, but the sub's captain, LCDR Frederic C. Lucas Jr., inexperienced, remained at his scope, watching the destroyer's approach. The OOD [officer of the deck] this day was LT Charles W. Rush Jr., who urged they dive.

"You are the diving officer. Do what you want," was the unorthodox reply from the inexperienced captain. Rush sent the boat deep, hoping to weather the inevitable depth charge barrage.

Earsplitting *booms* rocked the hull. Fittings popped, lights burst, and an ominous crack opened in the outboard diesel tank. Overhead the destroyer persisted. Barrage after barrage fell. For the next hour, then two, then three they fell.

One explosion breached an aft torpedo tube and flooding started. With many of the pumps out, chief electrician's mate John D. Rendernick organized a bucket brigade to move seawater forward where the bilge pumps still worked. Another deafening blast knocked the port motor off its mountings, and Rendernick and Chief Charles Odom used a hydraulic jack to lift the motor back in place. For hours the bombardment continued with uncanny accuracy! Damage mounted; survival seemed grim. Working in partially flooded spaces, the chiefs managed to force enough grease into the leaking torpedo tube to stem its inflow. But the attack continued, and Rush ordered the sub deeper. Explosions above her deck were damaging enough, but one under her keel would be fatal.

Past the 412-foot test-depth the sub sank. The bulkhead creaked, but not until 650 feet did Rush stop. Even here, her flooding required a 17° up-angle and two-thirds speed just to stay level. After twelve hours of unrelenting attack, Rush was able to move to the control room. Here he was shocked to find the captain paralyzed with fear, mumbling and praying in the corner. The XO [executive officer] sat as well, with his face in his hands. Worse, Rush discovered the sub had been cruising on a perfectly straight course, her diesel oil slick guiding the destroyers above!

Rush took the conn and ordered a 180 reverse. By doubling back under her own oil slick, *Billfish* managed an escape. Four hours later, with breathable air nearly gone, she surfaced to see the destroyers searching in the distance. Rush oversaw emergency repairs and got *Billfish* underway for Hawaii. A "gentleman's agreement" with Lucas kept his conduct quiet in exchange for his resignation from the submarine service. As a result, the heroic actions of that night were not revealed for decades.

* * *

Lieutenant Commander Lucas went on to distinguished service in the surface Navy of WWII.

Lieutenant Rush served out the war in submarines and remained on active duty until his retirement at the rank of captain in 1961. He went on to command the *Queenfish* (SS-393) in the Korean conflict. True to his gentleman's agreement, his heroism of this day did not come to light until decades after his retirement. On April 5, 2002, the eighty-five-year-old World War II veteran was awarded the Navy Cross. Odom and Rendernick (who died in December 2001) also received the Silver Star. On August 17, 2004, the Naval Submarine Training Center's Damage Control Wet Trainer in Pearl Harbor was named to honor Chief Electrician's Mate Rendernick.

In 2004, Captain Rush (Ret) published a novel, *Battle Down Under*, an account of the fictional submarine *Striker* during WWII. His novel borrows heavily from Rush's real-life experiences.

For further information, reference Keith Don, *War Beneath the Waves: A True Story of Courage and Leadership Aboard a World War II Submarine* (Penguin Publishing Group: New York, NY, 2010).

* * *

For the past twenty years, James Bloom has written one-page digest vignettes of events in naval history called "Today in Naval History." He can be reached at Navalist@aol.com.

USS *Puffer* (SS-268)

USS *Puffer* (SS-268) was a *Gato*-class submarine She was commissioned on April 27, 1943. *Puffer* earned nine battle stars for her World War II service.

Information taken from https://en.wikipedia.org/wiki/USS _Puffer_(SS-268)

O. L. FRITH
"Man Overboard"
Written by O. L. Frith
Reprinted from *Polaris* / December 2014

Puffer was on her seventh war patrol, and it was time to convert #4 fuel ballast tank (FBT) to a main ballast tank (MBT). Fleet submarines ran with an open flood port at the bottom of their tanks. As fuel was used, salt water replaced the fuel in the tank. Therefore, fuel floated on top of the salt water. When the FBT was empty, the fuel line was blocked off and the line was routed to a vent valve that could be operated from the control room. These blanks had to be done topside, in the superstructure between the hull and main deck.

Normally this was done at night, but because of the rough seas the captain decided to do the job in daylight hours at 1700 hours. The sighting of Japanese aircraft hampered the efforts several times. Work continued to be resumed each time, after diving and surfacing. Finally, at 1800 hours, work was started again on the conversion, even though waves were breaking over the main deck, then the captain took control of the submarine.

With overcast skies and dim light, I, O. L. Frith, Fireman First Class, was hit by a large wave. I was caught in a lifeline near the after gun mount momentarily. Hope gave way to despair as I was swept overboard.

The captain ordered, "All stop, left full rudder!" until the stern cleared me, while I struggled in the water. About this time, heavy clouds obscured the moon and total darkness descended. I had lost sight of the submarine, and things looked dark for me—real dark. I removed my shoes and other clothing that hindered me in the water. I conserved my strength and began to whistle.

Fortunately, the searchlight was still rigged on the bridge and had not flooded out. The captain turned the ship's control over to another, and he took a place on the after deck to help listen and look for me. I was heard off the port quarter, and the light was turned on me, but with the boat dead in the water it began to drift down sea past me. The boat was drifting faster than I could swim.

The captain ordered backing down on one propeller and going ahead on the other, to twist the stern upwind. At the same time, a swimmer was put into the water with a buoy to bring me on deck. Needless to say, it was a narrow escape. I received the following citation:

> *For heroic conduct in the performance of volunteer serves under extremely adverse conditions while serving aboard a U.S. Submarine in a combat area; fully comprehending the many dangers involved, Frith volunteered to undertake necessary work on the fuel system. Although exposed to the fury of a mountainous sea, he diligently carried out these special services until a large wave washed him overboard. His calm manner, fighting spirit, and presence of mind contributed much to his rescue nearly twenty minutes later. His conduct throughout was an inspiration to all with whom he served and in keeping with the highest traditions of the United States Naval Service.*
>
> — Ribbon Authorized, C. W. Nimitz, Fleet Admiral,
> U.S. Navy

THOMAS ADDISON METZ

Excerpts from a journal written on April 10, 1976

I was drafted into the U.S. Navy at Little Rock, Arkansas, on January 9, 1944, and was given six days' induction leave to complete personal business. I reported back to Little Rock on January 14 for transportation by troop train to the San Diego Naval Training Station for eight weeks' boot training. I was then placed in Company 44-049 about January 21, 1944.

We lived at Camp Decatur in eight-man huts. While we were in quarantine, we were given shots and haircuts. We learned how to store a mattress cover full of clothes in one seabag. The Navy had no razors or toothbrushes to issue us, and some of the boys didn't bring toiletry articles with them. So they began to look really wooly by the time they received a razor from home. I took the razor I had been issued in July 1940 by the CCC. I carried this razor halfway around the world, and I am still using it today (1976).

At camp we spent hours aiming an empty rifle at a target and snapping it; the Navy called this "snapping in." Later on, we did go to the rifle range out in the country near San Diego. There we used 03-A Army rifles and fired them at targets 200 yards away. At the prone and sitting positions and on rapid fire, I hit the bull's-eye almost every shot. But on standing position, single fire, I wasn't so good. I made a total score of 128 out of a possible 150. The 03-A3 Army rifles are the same ones the Army used during World War I. The Army used M-1 rifles during World War II, so the Navy inherited the older and slower bolt-action 03's. The firing range officer explained that the Navy always stays one war behind on rifles.

In July 1944, I bought $25 worth of quarters, went to a pay phone, and called Orvie Ruth Norwood in Hartford, Connecticut. When the quarters were used up, I had proposed to her and she accepted. Orvie rode the train from Hartford to Vallejo by herself. I've concluded in the past thirty-one years (1976) that women must have been ready to marry. Orvie stayed at the Hospitality House while we were getting our blood tests and completing our four-day waiting period so we could get married. We were married by a justice of the peace at City Hall. A man and woman from some of the other offices served as witness to the ceremony. I had Orvie's wedding ring in its box wrapped in paper and tied with a twine string, so it took me awhile to get it for the JP. After our wedding ceremony, we had our picture taken for the folks back home. For the next four months, we lived in furnished rooms on Carolina Street in Vallejo. Shore Patrolman

Frank Comerado and his wife, Grace, lived at the same rooming house. After Orvie and I decided to marry, I wrote Mrs. Norwood a letter telling of our decision. Her reply to me was, "Whatever Orvie decides is okay with me." I think my mother-in-law has been mostly pleased with me as a son-in-law, except in the areas of religion and politics.

By September 1944, it became apparent to me that if I was going to do the U.S. government any good in the Navy, I was going to have to go where the Japanese were. And the quickest and most efficient way to do that was on a fleet submarine headed for the Pacific.

A few days before Thanksgiving 1944, we loaded the boat with supplies, fuel, ammunition, food, water, and torpedoes. Then we headed for Pearl Harbor along a circle route up north near the Aleutians. I was still on KP and the sea was extremely rough all the way. I stayed seasick from the time we went under the Golden Gate Bridge until we walked ashore at Pearl Harbor. I had bleached out by this time till you could scarcely tell where the skin stopped and my white uniform started. I was so sick for so long that they talked of putting me off the boat for shore duty, but they decided to try me on lookout duty so I could get some fresh air and sunshine. I have always given Mr. Decker credit for that decision. But I am glad they kept me on the *Puffer*, for I got over my seasickness okay.

We were in Australia in July, and that is wintertime south of the equator. The weather was pretty and not too cool. The climate around Western Australia must be mostly arid. The timber I saw was a small and very scattered stand.

On our way to Subic Bay in the Philippines, we took two or three kinds of jungle disease vaccines plus Atabrine tablets for malaria. I never was able to figure these precautions out, because we never were allowed out of sight of our own ship. We tied up alongside a sub tender with lots of other subs and many surface ships.

About two or three days after arrival, a motor whale boat took some of us ashore to a sandy beach along the south side of the bay. The entertainment consisted of loafing in the sand and a wiener roast with cold drinks for lunch.

Sunday night, October 24, 1976: "The other night I awoke and couldn't go back to sleep. I thought of the good things we have and the freedom we have to enable us to enjoy these blessings. Then I remembered the terrible cost to our fellow Americans for us to keep this freedom. Some sacrificed their lives individually and freely. Others spent years in POW camps under deplorable conditions. Others were buried alive as their ships sank. Some of these lived three weeks or more in these sunken coffins. As I lay awake, so thankful for my good health, warm bed in which to rest, loved ones and good friends to enjoy, I wondered how I would have reacted if circumstances would have called me to make a sacrifice like those men. It always gives me butterflies in my stomach when I consider things like these."

* * *

Thomas Addison (T. A.) Metz S/N844-97-54, was born December 25, 1921. As of April 10, 1976, he lived at London, Arkansas, when he wrote these words in his journal and gave permission for them to be reprinted in the U.S. Submarine Veterans of WWII—Arkansas Diamond Chapter July 2006 newsletter.

* * *

From the *Dictionary of American Naval Fighting Ships*[5]:

---

[5] http://www.ibiblio.org/hyperwar///USN/ships/danfs/SS/ss268.html

USS *Puffer* (SS-268), Tom (T. A.) Metz. Photo courtesy of Mary Nida Smith.

Puffer got under way on their sixth war patrol December 16, operating in the Namsei Shoto area where she sank Coast Defense Vessel No. 42 on January 10, 1945. Before she arrived at Guam on January 17, she had damaged a destroyer, three freighters, and a tanker. By February 11, she was following patrols in Luzon Straits and South China sea, where she bombarded Pratas Island. The *Puffer* made an anti-sweep of the Wake Island area.

After refit at Midway, she departed on May 20, 1945, to the South China and Java seas on her eighth war patrol. In a surface sweep of the northern Bali coast, *Puffer* destroyed, by gunfire, two Japanese sea trucks and six landing crafts on July 5 and inflicted extensive damage to harbor installations at Chelukan Bawang Bawang and Buleleng, Bali. After a brief interval at Fremantle, she headed north on her last patrol in the Java Sea.

USS *Puffer* (SS-268) earned nine battle stars for her service in the Pacific Theater. Completing that patrol with the cessation of hostilities, *Puffer* headed for Subic Bay, then on to the United States, reaching San Francisco on October 15. In 1946, she returned to Hawaii, where she trained officers and men in submarine warfare until returning to San Francisco on March 19 for inactivation.

USS *Snapper* (SS-185)

USS *Snapper* (SS-185) was a *Salmon*-class submarine. She was commissioned on December 16, 1937. She received six battle stars for her World War II service.

Information taken from https://en.wikipedia.org/wiki/USS _Snapper_(SS-185)

MELVIN TOLBERT SMITH

As told to Mary Nida Smith

To realize what it meant to be a young submarine sailor during WWII, and what it still means today, take a step or more down the hatch inside of a submarine with a fourteen-year member of the "Silent Service." Melvin T. Smith's dedication to the U.S. Navy started June 2, 1943, at the age of seventeen when he signed up in Idaho, where his family had recently moved. Here's his story in his own words.

"I felt for the first time that I was special, entering a special place, and was honored to know I had a job to do as I entered my first submarine. I rode the *S-28* as a student for the Underground

USS *Snapper* (SS-185)

Sound training for one week to learn how to pick up and track ships by having a keen ear. It meant knowing the difference in sounds and being able to identify each one in the oceans and seas, such as the animals, enemy ships, boats, or friendly ships. After a week, the *S-28* went out to sea and never returned. I didn't go on the *S-28* because I had a bad toothache and was sent to the dentist. Another sailor took my place. In the meantime, I was on the relief crew for four months. I worked on boats in the yard and attended Sound and Radar School for a short time.

"In October 1943, I was transferred to the USS *Snapper* (SS-185), where I was assigned Sound and Radar watch. We had no screen to look at, only above water when we used radar. Sonar is sound—listening with your ears. Your ears are the devices that locate objects, enemy ships, and submarines underwater.

"Following overhaul and practice runs at Pearl Harbor on March 14, 1944, the *Snapper* with its crew departed to begin her ninth war patrol, conducted in the area of the Bonin Islands.

"One night after midnight, approximately ten days at sea, we made contact with a convoy of twelve ships. We tracked them for some time. At four in the morning we made radar approach, firing eight torpedoes with six hits. We sank three enemy ships. At 0400, everything broke loose.

"The convoy escort picked us up on their sound gear and proceeded to release depth charges against us the entire day. The layers of cork that lined the inside to prevent moisture were popping and flying all over the place. Sixty-watt lightbulbs cracked and exploded, causing glass fragments to fly—pricking our hide and clinging to our clothing and hair. We tried to pick them off each other the best we could, but at that time we had more serious concerns on our minds—not being killed at the enemy's hands. At that time we lost all our electrical sonar equipment except the JP, a manual train, which was my battle station. I was the only qualified operator aboard. [JP is the Navy term for sonic listening gear. The J means that it can be used for listening only. The second letter, P, indicates the model.]

"Captain W. W. Walker abandoned the conning tower to come to the torpedo room where I was operating. He spent the

USS *Snapper* (SS-185), Mel Smith and fellow crew members, Navy Day 1945. The war is over. Photo from the archives of Mel Smith.

USS *Snapper* (SS-185) crew on the first Navy Day after WWII ends. Photo from the archives of Melvin T. Smith.

entire day with me as I kept track of the three destroyers that were releasing the depth charges. I don't know how many charges were dropped that day. Someone had to hold a flashlight for me to see my instruments. The enemy was so close you could hear the depth charges click before the explosion. It sounded like a barrel filled with explosives.

"We were driven down and sitting at about a 35° angle. At that time the enemy's sound gear made contact with us, holding us down the entire day. Two of their ships would 'ping' on us, and three would make runs against us. They took turns doing this. Their depth charges knocked out both of our sound equipment units. The *Snapper* suffered substantial damage. We lost all power. Everything was shut down, and the temperature hovered around 115–120°. We finally surfaced at about 2200. After we got everything working, we crept away.

"Shortly after surfacing, the chief of the boat said the captain ordered that I be relieved from the watch list until we reached port. However, Captain W. W. Walker wanted me to qualify in submarines. I had to know about every man's job—how the submarine operated, down to every nut and bolt. Before, I wasn't trained in all aspects of being a submariner. When we got to Pearl, we stayed at the Royal Hawaiian Hotel for three weeks instead of the planned two weeks. The USS *Snapper* required more time to be repaired. On arriving at Pearl, we learned from other crews that they had heard we were lost at sea, as we were long overdue.

"When I returned aboard the *Snapper*, the yeoman informed me the captain had rated me Soundman Third Class, a Radioman Striker. I didn't know what a soundman was. I asked the chief radioman, and he didn't know either. He had to look it up, and he found it was a new rating. I was the first soundman in submarines.

"We proceeded on our tenth war patrol, where we were assigned air rescue (picking up downed pilots) at Truk Island. The second day on station, enemy aircraft fired on us and we lost one lookout. One of the guys lost a leg and an arm, and the captain had shrapnel in his head. We proceeded to the sub-tender in Majuro Island to transfer the wounded. Later, as we approached Midway, the water was so rough we had to circle the island for a week. All we had left to eat was hotcakes, and our fuel was running low. We had to refuel, refit, and take on supplies before we could head out on the next war patrol.

"Our eleventh war patrol started on September 5. We were sent to the area of the Bonin Islands. It was to be the *Snapper's* final war patrol. On October 1, we encountered two enemy vessels escorted by a small patrol craft. The *Snapper* crew fired two of her bow torpedoes at the large target and then shot at the smaller vessel. We took off to Iwo Jima to take up lifeguard station until October 18. We had to refuel, and soon after we sailed to the Sub

USS *Sea Leopard* (SS-483). Crew members ___, Mel Smith, Barney Wixom, and ___. Photo from the archives of Melvin T. Smith.

Base at Pearl Harbor, where we received orders for a yard overhaul at Mare Island Naval Shipyard in Vallejo, California. The USS *Snapper* received six battle stars for World War II service.

"Later, the *Snapper* was assigned to Sub Base in New London, Connecticut, to become a school boat. We stayed until November 1945, before we were assigned to Boston Navy Shipyard for decommission of the USS *Snapper* (SS-185).

"The *Snapper* was my first assignment on a boat, and at such a young age, the patrols left an everlasting impression on me. Ninth Patrol entitled me to wear the Submarine Combat Insignia. Tenth Patrol entitled me to wear the Submarine Combat Insignia with one star for two successful patrols and a campaign award—the American Asiatic-Pacific. Eleventh Patrol entitled me to wear the Submarine Combat Insignia, with two stars. I served on the following boats in my Navy career: the USS

USS *Snapper* (SS-185). Melvin T. Smith eighteen years old, Second Class Sonarman, with crew members in the mess hall, Pearl Harbor. Photo from the archives of Melvin T. Smith.

Quiliback (SS-424), USS *Sennet* (SS-408), USS *Sea Fox* (SS-402), and the USS *Sea Leopard* (SS-483).

"The U-505 German submarine was commissioned August 26, 1941. It was one of the most valued prizes of World War II. My job was to check out the sonar as I rode in it and out of New London, Connecticut. After years of inspections, the U-505 was moved into Chicago, Illinois, June 27, 1954, to the Museum of Science and Industry. I also checked out other German boats such as the *U-2513* and *U-3008*. They were spoils of war that were brought to the States after the war was over. They were new experimental submarines the Germans had just commissioned. The future United States Navy submarines were patterned after German submarines.

"In between boarding submarines, I decided to try service in the HS-7 Anti-Submarine Squadron for about three years, where I earned my 'Wings.'

"Before receiving an Honorable Discharge, I spent two years as a Navy Recruiter at Ontario, Oregon (1959–1962). One of my dress uniforms still hangs in my closet. To me it hangs like a special badge of courage.

"I have the honor to wear these medals received from my submarine service: Dolphins pin given to a submariner once he learns all aspects of the submarine and how it functions; Silver Star in Lieu of Bronze Stars for six Good Conduct Awards; American Campaign Medal; Asiatic-Pacific Campaign Medal; Victory Medal World War II; Philippine Liberation Ribbon; Korean Service Medal; and the National Defense Service Medal. I received the Aircrew Insignia while serving as an aircraft flight crew member in this command only. I am entitled to wear a bronze star for subsequent awards of the Good Conduct Medal (fifth award) for the period of service ending June 1, 1958, while serving in

USS *Snapper* (SS-185). Crew reunion in Las Vegas. Photo from the archives of Melvin T. Smith.

the Helicopter Anti-submarine Squadron SEVEN, CIO FLEET (1957–1959)."

* * *

The following is a Letter of Commendation to Melvin T. Smith SOC, 554 14 34, USN, from Commanding Officer H. M. Nelson, Helicopter Anti-submarine Squadron Seven:

> On 15 January 1957, while operating from the USS *Leyte*, one helicopter of this command with four persons aboard ditched in the vicinity of the carrier. At the time of the incident, you were Sonar Operator of *H04S-3 BUNC 138529*, which was airborne nearby. Immediately after the ditching, you acted as hoist operator in the rescue of one of the crewmen, despite repeated electrical shocks, which you received as a result of a short circuit in the hoist system. An HU-2 helicopter rescued the two pilots and the other crewmen. The expiation and efficient manner in which you and the pilot, LTJG Murry H. Wright, USN, performed this mission demonstrated a high degree of training and skill on the part of both the pilot and crew, and is considered to be in keeping with the high traditions of the Navy. This letter will be made a permanent part of your record.

> —H. M. Nelsen, Commander,
> U.S. Navy Commanding Officer.

* * *

Officers of submarines on which Melvin T. Smith served:

USS *Snapper* (SS-184) Commanding Officer William W. Walker and Commanding Officer Captain Murphy.

USS *Sea Fox* (SS-402) Commanding Officer Ira Dye, CDR, USN.

USS *Sea Leopard* (SS-483) Commanding Officer L. J. Goulet, LCDR, USN.

USS *Quillback* (SS-424) One of the first commanders was R. P. Nicholson.

USS *Sennet* (SS-408) Commanding Officer Captain Robert Clark.

* * *

As of this writing, Melvin T. Smith, STC (SS) USN-RET, native of northwest Arkansas, is a member of the Holland Club, the Submarine Veterans of WWII, and is a plank-owning member of the United States Submarine Veterans Twin Lakes Base.

Christmas Below the Sea

Mary Nida Smith

Shut off from the outside world,
deep, deep below the sea,
thoughts of survival
housed in small quarters.
The cook roasts a turkey
to celebrate this special season.
Fifteen minutes, time out to eat,
back to the work station,
keeping watch deep below
or above the unpredictable seas.
No time to remember Christmas.
A moment of weak emotions,
a difference between life or death.
Holiday emotions are hidden
deep inside each man
who chose to serve aboard
a World War II submarine.

* * *

Written by the author of this book as her husband, Melvin T. Smith, SO1, WWII veteran, who spent sixteen years on submarines, shared his feelings about Christmas.

USS *Tullibee* (SS-284)

USS *Tullibee* (SS-284) was a *Gato*-class submarine. She was commissioned on February 15, 1943. During her fourth war patrol, she sunk herself when one of her torpedoes ran a circular course and struck the submarine.

Information taken from https://en.wikipedia.org/wiki/USS _Tullibee_(SS-284)

USS *Tullibee* (SS-284) Commanding Officer Charles Frederic Brindupke (1908–1944). Photo from www.oneternalpatrol.com.

CLIFF KUYKENDALL

"Sole survivor of USS *Tullibee* speaks about being a POW"

Written by Patrick Ochs, November 5, 2014

Permission given by reporter Patrick Ochs and the editor of the *Sun Herald*

OCEAN SPRINGS, Mississippi—The last thing Cliff Kuykendall remembers hearing before the explosion was a crewmate saying, "Well, there they go. We'll see what happens now."

"We found out about twenty seconds later," Kuykendall said Monday. "Boom!"

When Kuykendall came to—possibly a few minutes later, he's not sure—he watched helplessly as his submarine, the USS *Tullibee* (SS-284), slowly sank into the Pacific Ocean and out of sight.

"I thought, *Oh my God, I just lost my home*," he said. "It was a long way from there to Wichita Falls, Texas."

Kuykendall, the 2014 Gulf Coast Veterans Day Parade grand marshal, was a nineteen-year-old submariner in the early hours of March 26, 1944, when the *Tullibee* launched two torpedoes meant for a Japanese transport ship. Instead, the torpedoes ran a circular route and struck the submarine.

He was the lone survivor of a crew of eighty.

"The concussion was terrific. I was on the starboard during lookout. It was a real dark night, drizzling. I was almost unconscious," he recalled as he stood in front of the USS *Tullibee* memorial in Ocean Springs. "I remember looking down and I could see the stern of the submarine gradually go below the waves. Those

USS *Tullibee* (SS-284) portside view, under way off the Mare Island Navy Yard, California, April 2, 1943. USN photo #2235-43, courtesy of Darryl L. Baker.

World War II diesel submarines were 312 feet long, and I must have been way up there in the air, I don't know. When I came to, I was submerged in the ocean. I fought my way to the surface. I had swallowed so much water that I could taste salt and diesel fuel for at least a year after that."

Kuykendall said he could hear voices for about ten minutes after he regained consciousness. Then nothing.

He floated for several hours alone, except for an empty Sunkist orange crate that bumped into him.

He credited his shipmate Louis Joseph Hieronimus for saving his life. Hieronimus had forced him to take a lifebelt before going on lookout. The partially inflated life belt kept him afloat long enough to be spotted.

Unfortunately, it wasn't by Americans.

About 1000 hours, he saw a destroyer coming in his direction, flying the rising sun flag. "They made a circle around me, to my starboard, and opened up with the machine gun, firing at me," he said. "Fortunately, they never got a lethal shot in, but bullets were flying all over the place."

The Japanese brought him aboard, pulling him up with a fish net because he was too weak to climb aboard. That's when he had his third brush with death in less than twenty-four hours.

A Japanese officer holding a sword called him a coward for not drowning himself rather than being captured. The officer swung the sword over Kuykendall's head four times, missing each time.

"Each time he swung it—there were two Japanese sailors on either side of me holding me up—I collapsed and fell to the deck and the sword passed over my head," he said. "I did that intentionally because I knew if that sword hit my neck it would chop my head off."

A short time later, Kuykendall heard something in Japanese over the PA system and the harassment stopped—for the time being.

He was dragged into a deck house and tossed onto a mat.

"Another Japanese sailor came in who was carrying a small cup of sweet tea in his hand," he said. "He lifted my head and was giving me this sweet tea. He said in English, 'Don't worry, everything will be all right.' I said, 'Well, they're not all alike.'"

He was taken to a small seaplane base among the Palau Islands. Eventually, he was tied to a tree atop a hill while Americans bombed the island as part of Operation Desecrate. After three days of abuse tied to the tree, he was put into a foxhole behind a Japanese navy commander's house.

"Two days later, the owner of the house came up and got me and they took me back to the dock. I could see all of these hangars had been leveled and it made me feel good. He could speak English. Well, he saved my life. I know he did. They would have killed me if it hadn't been for him," Kuykendall said, re-enacting several captors punching him while he was tied up. "He took me out on the dock. A Japanese navy plane landed and he told me, 'There you go. Good luck.' Just like that. I looked at him and said, 'Sir, good luck to you. I hope you make it.' He said, 'I'll need it.'"

The next seventeen months or so, Kuykendall bounced among labor camps until World War II ended.

His final days as a captive, he worked in a copper mine in Ashio.

He recalled food rations increasing and American planes flying overhead.

"They were sending out fighters to locate all of the prison camps so they could drop them food, because they knew we were probably starving," he said.

When he returned to Texas, Kuykendall wrote letters to seventy-nine families, telling them what happened to the crew of the *Tullibee*. He would stare at the ceiling at night and try to figure out how he survived so many brushes with death.

"I'd say, 'I can't figure this out. How did this happen?' That went on for a couple of months. 'Why little ole me?' I suddenly realized that if I kept doing that I'd just worry myself to death. I had to stop. I never did figure it out. I've never been superstitious in my whole life—and I'm still not. What is, is. To this very day, like I have told people, I'm just lucky."

* * *

On August 25, 2001, *Tullibee* Base of Mississippi was chartered.

* * *

Patrick Ochs can be reached at pochs@sunheard.com.

USS *Blenny* (SS/AGSS-324)

USS *Blenny* (SS/AGSS-324) was a *Balao*-class submarine. *Blenny* was commissioned on June 27, 1944 and reported to the Pacific Fleet.

Between November 10, 1944, and August 14, 1945, *Blenny* conducted four war patrols in the Java and South China Seas, sinking eight Japanese vessels totaling 18,262 tons. In addition, she is credited with destroying more than 62 miscellaneous Japanese small craft by gunfire, and rescuing a boarding party lost by the *Cod* (SS-224) when that boat had to make an emergency dive. She received four battle stars for her World War II service and one battle star for her Korean war service.

Information taken from https://en.wikipedia.org/wiki/USS _Blenny_(SS-324)

111

HOWARD D. ECKHART

Written in 2006 by Robert D. Wilcox

Reprinted with permission by Wilcox and *50plus Senior News*

Lt. Howard "Howie" Eckhart grew up in Hopeland, near Brickerville, Pennsylvania. When the war broke out in 1941, he was a seventeen-year-old sophomore at Franklin and Marshall College. "All the men were going off to war," he says, "so I figured I better go, too." The choices he made after that brought him into the most dangerous service of the war.

He joined the Navy. After boot camp, he chose electronics, which got him six months of electronics school at Treasure Island in San Francisco, studying radar and sonar, and it earned him a rank of First Class Petty Officer Electronics Technician. There were 430 in his class. Thirty-six volunteered for submarine service, and two were picked. He was one of the two. Why had he picked submarines? "Because you get twice as much pay as in a surface billet, that's why," he explains. "Also, you come back in one piece or not at all."

Wasn't he pretty young to be doing that kind of dangerous work? "Well," he says, "the average age of everybody on our submarine was nineteen and a half. There were lots of kids my age." It was later determined by the military that the percentage of teenage deaths among submariners in WWII was the highest of any service.

From Treasure Island, Howie was next sent to Groton, Connecticut, where he became one of the first three crewmen assigned to the brand new submarine, USS *Blenny*. In April 1944, he rode her down the ways, thus becoming "plank owner," a distinction for the original crew members of a Navy vessel.

USS *Blenny* (SS-324) sliding down the launching ways at Electric Boat Company, Groton, Connecticut, April 9, 1944. Photo Courtesy of Frank Toon, Coquille, Oregon.

The *Blenny* could make 22.5 knots on the surface and 8.75 knots submerged. Her safe diving depth was 400 feet. Howie was the main radar operator.

After training in New London and Newport, the *Blenny* set off in August for Key West, for training in the fleet sound school. The sub transited the Panama Canal in September, and reached Pearl Harbor the next month. In November, she left for her assigned patrol area in the waters off the coast of Luzon in the Philippines.

On the way, they fired a torpedo at a Japanese escort vessel. It missed but brought them a severe but unsuccessful depth-charge attack. Five days later, a low-flying enemy plane dropped two bombs, which just missed them.

USS *Blenny* (SS-324)

Howie explains that we had cracked the Japanese code before the war, and that helped greatly in directing subs to targets. In one major engagement, they sank a Japanese troop transport carrying 5,000 troops. And on Christmas Day, they were directed to a convoy of four tankers protected by three destroyers. They sank three of the four tankers, then rode out a fierce depth-charge attack. Howie explains, "The Japanese thought we could go only to a depth of 200 feet, so they set their charges for that depth. Actually, we could go to 400 feet, so while we got really battered, they didn't get us. But when one of those charges would go off, it sounded like the loudest clap of thunder you ever heard."

What about life aboard the sub when they weren't in combat? Were the quarters really tight? "Well," he says with a grin, "my bunk was over a stack of six torpedoes, right under the curve of the hull. To turn over, I had to slide out, turn over, then slide back in." How about the food? "Oh, it was great. The Navy spent twice as much per man for our food as they did for sailors aboard surface vessels. Our food was unbelievable. We had shrimp, prime rib, you name it." Did it get boring? "Not really," he says, "but we played a lot of cards—hearts, cribbage, that kind of stuff. The Navy provided us with three silver cribbage boards."

How were they able to sink so many enemy ships—sixty-three by Navy records? "Well, toward the end of the war, we were patrolling off the coast of French Indo China, and the Japanese had had all of their transport vessels sunk. They were forced to transport men and war material in junks and sampans. We would surface and use our five-inch guns and machine guns to attack and sink them. Once, we sank an unbelievable eight in one day!"

The *Blenny* also rescued a boarding party lost by the USS *Cod*.

The *Blenny* returned to San Francisco after the war, and Howie was discharged and returned home. He went back to finish up at Franklin & Marshall College, then attended dental school at the University of Pennsylvania, staying in the Naval Reserve while there and earning his commission. He graduated in 1953 as a dental surgeon. After five years with another oral surgeon, he opened his own office in Lancaster in 1958.

He had always wanted to fly, so he signed up for flight school on the day he was discharged from the Navy. He owned a number

USS *Blenny* (SS-324), Howard D. Eckhart

of single- and twin-engine aircraft over the years and earned ratings for single, multi-engine, instrument, and flight instructor with 7,500 hours of flying time. The Eckharts are a flying family. His wife, Jessie (the daughter of the late, legendary Lancaster airman, Jessie Jones), is a noted flier with 9,000 flying hours. Eckhart was a member of the Lancaster Chapter of the Military Officers Association.

USS *Sea Cat* (SS/AGSS-399)

USS *Sea Cat* (SS/AGSS-399) was a *Balao*-class submarine. *Sea Cat* was commissioned on May 16, 1944. She earned three battle stars for her World War II service.

Information taken from https://en.wikipedia.org/wiki/USS _Sea_Cat_(SS-399)

WAYNE B. GOODENOW

From information submitted to Mary Nida Smith

Wayne B. Goodenow ET1 (SS) USN was assigned to *Sea Cat* in 1944. Commodore Robert R. McGregor was in command. It was a typical 311-foot WWII submarine loaded with ten torpedo tubes—six forward, four aft—and it carried a total of twenty-four torpedoes. Included with the range was the addition of two five-inch guns with the range of seven nautical miles. *Sea Cat* was pre-tested to dive 400 feet, but most captains on war patrols never hesitated to exceed the pre-tested dive by 50 percent, to protect their boat and crew from the enemy. It had a crew of sixty-five enlisted men and seven officers.

Following training in Hawaiian waters, in October *Sea Cat* sailed on their first war patrol to the South China Sea. Their orders read: "Carry out unrestricted submarine warfare. Seek out and sink enemy shipping." *Sea Cat* joined a wolf pack with three sister ships, the USS *Pampanito* (SS-383), USS *Pipefish* (SS-388), and USS *Sea Raven* (SS-196).

Throughout that patrol they experienced long periods below, "silent running." They had to dive deep for protection from the ruthless depth-charge attacks by three destroyer escorts protecting enemy tankers.

"During this time, everything was shut down and the temperature inside could exceed 130. We were dripping wet. Air was tight and we could barely breathe. This is the way we sometimes sat for hours. I guess this is where they got the phrase 'silent running.' We couldn't make a sound. We sure didn't want the enemy to pick up our location," said Goodenow.

Many times while on patrol with the wolf pack, the battles took place below, above, and everywhere. It was difficult to calculate approximately how many enemy ships were destroyed, if any. After *Sea Cat* had been at sea for sixty-one days, it went to Guam for refit, repairs, and fuel.

Their second war patrol started in February 1945, in the East China Sea, where it carried out its patrol again as part of a wolf pack, with USS *Segundo* (SS-398) and USS *Razorback* (SS-394).

"On this run, we accidentally encountered a minefield. We heard the steel cables that held the mines suspended scrape along our hull. Talk about sudden fear setting in! This was it! We moved slowly with great caution until we were safely out of that area," said Goodenow.

"After two months at sea, we arrived at Midway in March for repairs, supplies, and a much-needed rest. While on patrol there was little time for resting."

They had about a month layover at Midway before heading out to the Yellow Sea. This time it was with a wolf pack of six other submarines. They had orders to knock out Japanese shipping. *Sea Cat* sank 400 tons of enemy vessels with their five-inch guns, and they picked up two survivors from the sinking ships, whom they held for questioning.

On August 6, 1945, *Sea Cat* headed from Pearl Harbor to the Kurils on its fourth patrol. Upon arriving, they learned the war had ended. They were ordered to Tokyo Bay, where the formal surrender ceremony took place on September 2, 1945. The following day they were dispatched to Guam, where they arrived on the September 7. After a brief stay, they headed home for the States.

"It was hard to realize the war was over and we had survived. By the time I departed from Guam, I had ridden this same submarine 117,000 nautical miles and made 717 dives," recalled Goodenow. "The most important statistic of all . . . we surfaced 717 times."

* * *

Wayne B. Goodenow ET1 (SS) USN was an active member of the Submarine Veterans of World War II, and lived in Hot Springs Village, Arkansas.

Thank God that I'm a Sub-Vet's Wife

Irma Goodenow

Now as I laid me down to sleep
I tossed and turned and counted sheep.
I prayed about the things in life.
Thank God that I'm a sub-vet's wife.

If not for him, I'd not be here
to make friends from far and near.
This sailor man changed my life.
Thank God that I'm a sub-vet's wife.

As Silent Service they are known—
with a special bond that's all their own.
They tell their tales and sometimes jive.
Thank God that I'm a sub-vet's wife.

Now when they heard the klaxon's dive
(their job was not from nine to five),
for each of us they gambled life.
Thank God that I'm a sub-vet's wife.

Let's not forget when we take roll
those gallant men still on patrol,
and who've since departed life.
They too once had a sub-vet wife.

And then I turned and watched him sleep.
"Dear Lord," I prayed, "my sub-vet keep.
We've been a pair through love and strife."
Thank God that I'm a sub-vet's wife.

USS *Boarfish* (SS-327)

USS *Boarfish* (SS-327) was a *Balao*-class submarine. *Boarfish* was commissioned on September 23, 1944. She received one battle star for her World War II service.

Information taken from https://en.wikipedia.org/wiki/USS _Boarfish_(SS-327)

WILLIAM DREHER
As told to Mary Nida Smith

The USS *Boarfish* was commissioned on September 23, 1944, at New London, Connecticut, with Cdr. Royce L. Gross in command. William Dreher QMIC (SS) was one of the crew that was assigned to the boat. Several sea trials and practice runs were conducted before sailing on December 2, 1944, to Pearl Harbor. At Pearl they received their first war patrol assignment in an area off the coast of Indochina.

"At that time, war targets were very rare. We were all anxious to put our training into use," said Dreher. "Patrolling submerged during the day and surfacing at night with no contacts was very boring."

"On the morning of December 30, our radar made contact with two ships close to shore. We quietly waited until evening. Under the cover of darkness, we started our approach. As we moved closer, our radar picked up two more contacts close to our two main targets. We determined them to be escort vessels. Our radar reported interference, which indicated the escort also had radar."

The USS *Boarfish* continued to move toward the two ships with caution. Suddenly, within one mile of their targets, they heard a loud explosion overhead. "Apparently their escorts were able to pick up our direction and range on their radars, for they started firing their antiaircraft shells over us," said Dreher.

Captain Gross informed the crew it would be impossible to get within firing range while shells exploded overhead. He asked for Dreher to get out the coastal area charts. After taking time to study them, he stated there was a small cove offshore approximately forty miles beyond the target ships and their escorts. The captain thought if they could get into the cove, the targets might take the shortcut and go straight rather than follow the shoreline.

The captain ordered full speed ahead, hoping to reach the cove before daybreak. They reached the cove safely and stayed submerged in approximately eighty feet of water. The executive officer asked the captain how he planned on getting out with the escorts blocking the exit. He replied, "I don't plan on getting out. Those two ships are worth more to the war effort than this old submarine."

They sat there in what is known as "silent running." Everything was shut down except emergency lights, and one-third of the crew were at their stations. It was difficult for the other two-thirds of the crew to wait it out, for they had nothing to do to distract their minds from thinking of the danger.

"This is when reality set in," said Dreher. A glimpse of sadness showed in his eyes as he continued. "I started to think of my wife whom I had just married three months before, and of our baby she was carrying. Would I ever see them? Then, I quickly pulled myself out of these thoughts. As a protective device, I remembered this was war and we had a job to be done."

Soon after, the sun rose, reflecting on the water, and both targets came into view. As the crew had hoped, the vessels took the shortcut and did not follow the shoreline.

The forward torpedo room was equipped with both the newer electric torpedoes and the older steam torpedoes. When the ships passed by, the crew fired three torpedoes at each one. Then the *Boarfish* immediately lowered to the bottom of the sea, rigged for silence, and waited for the depth charges. Sonar reported several explosions, so they sat quietly and waited. To their surprise they didn't hear any depth charges nearby. They heard them off in the distance. The *Boarfish* sonar couldn't pick up noise from the screws, so that meant the escorts were not close.

The explosions continued for about four hours. Then, suddenly, everything was quiet. The *Boarfish* waited it out at the bottom of the cove. Under darkness it surfaced, then headed out to sea and deeper water.

"Luck was with us, or it could have been that all the lookouts on the escorts were looking out to sea, knowing there were other submarines in that area," said Dreher as he continued to ponder over what happened that morning years ago. "When we heard explosions in back of us, we looked around to see what was happening. We spotted the wake from a steam torpedo that had missed its target. Because the wake was outboard of the ship, the Japs may have thought they were being fired from outboard. All I know is the Japs were dropping depth charges in deep water while we were resting quietly on the bottom at eighty feet."

Later, the USS *Boarfish* was credited with sinking the 6,968-ton *Enki Maru* and damaging a 7,000-ton ship that was later destroyed by aircraft. "When I look back on that war patrol, I think I owe my life to the steam torpedoes. I am glad it's behind me," commented Dreher.

The USS *Boarfish* made four war patrols in the South Sea, Java Sea, and Gulf of Siam.

* * *

Note from the author: At the time that William H. Dreher QMIC (SS) gave me his story, he resided in South Milwaukee, Wisconsin. Dreher also served aboard the USS *Tinosa* and the USS *Guitarro* (SS-363). Below he shares what he believed happened while he was a crew member aboard the *Guitarro*. It may not be exactly as written in the official report.

In January 1943, when the USS *Guitarro* was conducting sea trials in Lake Michigan, prior to the government accepting it from the Manitowoc shipyard, it developed a problem with the diving alarm on the bridge. When the water leaked in with the temperature around 10°F, it froze and set off the alarm. It was a single blast, which the captain gave orders to ignore. The electrician cut the power to it, and they returned to port with instructions to have it repaired along with other problems they had found.

After the repairs had been made, another trial run was conducted in the cold waters of Lake Michigan, with temperatures around zero. After the first dive, they were ready to surface. All officers were in the conning tower except a junior officer who was stationed at the diving controls. When the surfacing alarm went off and they had reached the surface, QMIC Dreher opened the conning latch to let the captain go first. When the captain made it to the bridge, the diving alarm went off the second time. He immediately yelled over the speaker, "Do not dive! Do not dive!"

Everyone heard it except the man on the diving station vent valves and the junior officer. The man at the vent controls had not waited for the second alarm as was required, and he immediately opened the valves.

Instantly, the captain heard the air escaping from the tanks as he dropped down through the hatch. Before he hit the bottom, the submarine sank below the surface and the ice-cold water began pouring through the hatch. The officers tried to grasp the lanyard to close the hatch. "I closed the lower conning tower hatch. Within seconds, the water was up to our necks," said Dreher.

When the water poured through the lower tower hatch, the crew member at the valves knew something was wrong. He started blowing all tanks to get the submarine to the surface. The captain ordered the drain values to be opened. The water was not going down fast enough, so he informed the officer below to open the hatch. "No, the ship will not sink!" he yelled back. By this time everyone in the conning tower was cold and wet. Dreher quickly dove down in the water, where he lifted the hatch, allowing the water to drop below.

Since all the officers were wet, the captain went up on the bridge to stand watch until the other officers changed into dry clothes. By the time the captain was relieved, his heavy clothing was frozen stiff. He had to be helped down the hatch, as he couldn't bend his legs.

"We were fortunate it was freshwater. There was little damage to the radar and torpedo controls. Everything had to be checked over and the faulty dive button replaced," recalled Dreher.

On submarine duty, mistakes couldn't be tolerated, no matter how small. The men depended on each other to survive below the sea. But war was warm where young men with little training, or none at all, were rushed out to sea on war patrol.

"The junior officer below was removed from ship's crew, but I don't remember what happed to the crew member on the vent valves. It was a hard lesson many of us on the *Guitarro* remembered: Do not open the vents until the second alarm is heard."

USS *Guavina* (SS/SSO/AGSS/ AOSS-362)

USS *Guavina* (SS/SSO/AGSS/AOSS-362) was a *Balao*-class submarine. *Guavina* was commissioned on December 23, 1943. She received five battle stars for her World War II service.

From January 23 to March 5, 1945, the USS *Guavina* (SS-362) spent her fifth patrol as part of a wolf pack, with USS *Pampanito* (SS-383), USS *Becuna* (SS-319), and the USS *Blenny* (SS-324) in the South China Sea. They sank two tankers, and the USS *Guavina* experienced one of the worst depth charges of World War II.

The following is from a chapter from the book, *Pacific Patrol: A WWII Submarine Saga*, self-published in 1993 by Marion Shinn. He tells his experiences in his own words on behalf of the fifth war patrol of the USS *Guavina* (SS-362) in February 1945.

MARION SHINN

Written by Marion Shinn

From his book, *Pacific Patrol: A WWII Submarine Saga*

It was Valentine's Day 1944, when our boat arrived at Cam Ranh Bay, off the coast of what was then French Indochina, but love and red hearts were far from our minds. The weather was still bad, but the waves were not as vicious as we experienced here the previous December. The electronic surveillance from the beach still caused interference on our radar screens, but it was not persistent. The captain felt reasonably safe patrolling close to the beach. There were no little patrol boats, only low flying float planes continuing to search. They kept us submerged most of the time.

Our assigned patrol station was familiar. It was from Cam Ranh past Phan Rang, to Padaran Cape, a forty- or fifty-mile coastline. For several consecutive days we raced to battle stations at 0730 hours. This was breakfast time, and we left our plates of food on the tables. The captain made no attacks. The possible targets were either the tiny boats from the local ports or big ones that were too far away.

On February 20 at 0730, the mess cook had breakfast ready, and we had just started eating. The battle stations bell rang, *Bong, bong, bong* throughout the boat—just as it had for four days. Many of us went halfhearted to our battle stations. I thought a cold breakfast wasn't the way to start the day.

I proceeded at a reasonable rate to my battle station in the forward torpedo room and put on my headset to the JP sound gear. As I rotated the sensitive listening head, I could clearly hear the sound of the screws from a passing ship. The sound became closer and closer until it appeared to be directly overhead. I thought it was odd there was no comment or action from the conning tower.

I relaxed for a moment, thinking maybe the ship had left the area. Suddenly, I sat upright as orders came from the conning tower: "Stand by forward." I rapidly spun the sound head around, straining to hear the activity above the sea. Suddenly, the captain shouted, 'Fire one, Fire two, Fire three, Fire four!'

We listened to the rapid first thunderous explosion, the second, and the third as the torpedoes hit their target. Next order followed with an urgent, 'Dive with hard rudder.' Without delay we hit the bottom, and a thumping sound filled the boat, followed by a long *whoosh* as we slid along the sandy bottom. Wild, crazy thoughts raced through my mind: *What was up there? Will the silt and mud rise to the top to give away our location?* For a moment, I held my breath as I waited for the depth charges to explode. I waited. I wondered what happened. Nothing!

I was extremely grateful we had the new JP sound head. It was installed in Perth less than a month ago. The new JP projected from the deck and the old sound heads pushed through the bottom of the hull.

I felt like we were a bottom fish. Fleet submarines were named after fish during World War II. The guavina is a small tropical bottom fish that reputedly buries its head in the mud in times of danger. Like our namesake, our boat repeatedly lived up to that reputation.

The depth gauges read 130 feet. We rigged for 'silent running.' All motors including the power fans, air conditioners, and the bow and stern planes were stopped. The only equipment moving was JP sound gear. I rotated it quietly by hand. The churning screws on the surface ship were clearly audible. It was only moments before the depth charges started falling.

Before our attack, the Japanese convoy consisted of a large tanker, a small freighter, and destroyers following the coastline. The two merchantmen were only a few hundred feet from the beach. The destroyers were trying to protect the other two ships loaded with cargo, as it hovered between the merchantmen. The other destroyer was parallel and seaward of the two cargo ships. The third was bringing up the rear. When the battle stations sounded, the five vessels were moving toward us. The captain waited quietly. The lead destroyer passed directly over us.

The action started when our position was between the outboard destroyer and the merchantman. We were in a very dangerous position. The destroyer was lightly to our port side. She was between us and the open sea. Even before the torpedoes reached the tanker (later identified as the 8,673-ton *Eiyo Maru*), Captain Lockwood took evasive action. He ordered a hard rudder slipping under the outboard destroyer and slid to a stop on the bottom.

After the noise and turbulence caused by the exploding torpedoes subsided, my task on the sound gear was to follow the screw noises of the four remaining ships. This information went to the conning tower through the sound-powered phones. It seemed natural to lower my voice to a whisper. The surviving freighter slowly moved away from the attack site, as one of the destroyers followed. The two remaining warships (destroyers) started to search for us in a very methodical way.

One destroyer pinged its sound gear as the other one made a run over the location. Moments after the whistling sound of the racing propellers passed, a string of depth charges explored over us. The destroyers would trade places. The second warship would shake us with another string of charges.

After taking the second merchantman to a safe anchorage, the third destroyer returned to join in the search for us. The destroyers dropped many depth charges. When that didn't work to locate us, they tried other tactics. All three warships stopped dead in the water at the same time, apparently listening for a slight noise from us. They were hoping someone on our boat would sneeze or cough, make some kind of noise, or the movement from some of our equipment might be audible.

Each set of screws of the propeller on an enemy ship has a distinctive sound. However, it was frustrating keeping track of each boat separately. I would hand rotate the sound head back and forth, following the progress of each ship. The conning tower was kept informed of the direction each destroyer was traveling. The listening gear did not give information to determine distance. It would only be estimated by the level of the sound.

Words cannot express the feelings and emotions that surged through my mind while waiting helplessly. Many of the crew stretched out motionless on the deck on their departments. From my position only, the men in the forward torpedo room and ward room were visible. Some were emotionless, but most had a look of fear on their faces. One man sat down on the floor and started to giggle, but soon brought it under control.

Bob Winklemann, a lookout and mechanic, was with me for relief. The other man, assigned to relieve our watch, broke out in a cold sweat. He carried a large towel around his neck to wipe off the perspiration, but the water dripped faster than he could wipe it. Fear and emotions were strong. He reacted violently when he started bumping his head against the bulkhead. He was eased away to another part of the boat and never returned to relieve us on the sound gear. The listening gear was probably one of the best places to be during the battle stations. During those stressful hours there was work to do. Thinking about the possibility and probability of death was put aside.

We tracked the sound of the three destroyers for about four hours. Finally, they moved away and left us alone. I was restless and hoped we could, and would, ease out of this hot spot. The captain was cautious and patient. Suddenly at about noon there was a new sound in the water. A destroyer came toward us off the port side at high speed, possibly thirty-five knots, pinging furiously. The screws whined like a police siren. Inside our boat it was almost deafening.

A few minutes later, another fast moving warship passed over us. It dropped six depth charges extremely close to us. Several lightbulbs in the overhead broke, and the glass shattered on the deck below. There was faint sound of running water. A compensating water line broke, and the sea was flooding the mess hall. The auxiliary man quietly slipped over and reached into the bilge, where he turned a safety valve to close off the line. Those of us in the forward room did not know of the danger until afterward.

All of the crew remained in the resting position until 1500 hours. The enemy ships were no longer searching for us. The last noises had been at about noon—1200 hours. Our depth gauge was 138 feet. If the gauge was accurate, it meant our hull was pushed in the mud eight feet. The only way to pull ourselves out was to give the boat an upward jerk. This was done by blowing the water from the forward ballast tank. There was a tiny bit of movement while the ballast tanks were blown. The tanks were flooded again and the process was repeated.

After a few of these seesaw movements, we were free. The water moving out of the tanks forced mud off the bottom to create turbulence. The risk of giving away our position was one we could not avoid. The screws were set to move very slowly as we eased off the bottom to move quietly to safer water.

The crew began to move around, assessing the damage. Ninety-eight depth charges were dropped on us during the attack, more than all our other previous war patrol runs combined. Sitting quiet and motionless on the bottom during those frightening hours, many of us thought about our past unrighteous acts. It was a time to consider whether submariners really possessed immortality.

None of us were in the mood for the cold breakfast we missed. Food was not very appealing at that moment. Suddenly, a horrible smell filled the galley and mess hall. The cook had a large turkey thawing that he had taken out before the attack. The oppressive heat had thawed it quickly. Rotten turkey gives off the most putrid odors one can generate. Soon as the air system started generating, the smell quickly moved through the submarine.

For nearly an hour, our course was east toward the open sea. When the captain felt we were out of the danger zone, we were given the order to surface. A long line of men waited to get to the surface when the hatch opened. The regular lookouts went up first. The cook was not far behind. He carried the putrid turkey to the bridge, where he tossed it into the sea. Following were men from every department. We swarmed on deck to survey the damage. We didn't stay on topside long. Exploring depth charges were faintly audible from the direction we had come. Apparently, the destroyers had gone to a nearby port to load up more depth charges. We had timed our move just right.

The concussion from the explosions caused extensive damage to the boat topside. The four-inch steel SJ radar mast would not rotate. The SD radar had a couple of vacuum tubes shattered, and the radio was down. Dimples in the hull and misaligned shafts could not be fixed at sea. We limped forty or fifty miles into open sea, where we could check the damage more closely. It was indeed extensive. We were lucky to be alive.

For four or five days we stayed in open water at the east end of our assigned patrol area. Crews from each department tried to repair topside damage. The bearings on the radar mast were relaxed enough to allow the damaged four-inch pipe to rotate. The transmitter operated, but most of the energy—probably 60 percent—was lost on the way to the antenna. By the process of elimination, it was decided the problem was the resistance cards in the mast. The replacement parts were about the size of half a playing card, but more fragile.

Willoughby, Stone, and I took out tools topside to attack the problem. Climbing to the top of the periscope shears was not easy. It was even more difficult to pull the radar mast head. The sea was rough. The boat pitched and rolled. The movement was more exaggerated from our position on top the shears. It was hard to hang on. It took all the strength of one arm to cling to the mast. Keeping the wrench on the moving bolts high overhead was difficult and frustrating. Coordinating the efforts of three men hanging in space did not come easy. As we lowered the fragile resistance cards into their place, a big wave went over us. The cards were shattered against the metal side of the masthead. We screwed the mast back together and waited for another day.

The following night, the sea was a little less violent. Our location was still in the heart of enemy territory, but something had to be done. Again, Willoughby, Stone, and I went topside, this time with our last set of resistance cards from the spare parts box. Since it was very dark, we carried a flashlight with a red filter. The light was a concern, for there was a chance the dim glow would be sighted by the enemy. The lookouts kept their binoculars pointed toward the hostile sea. They frequently glanced up to see if the three of us were still there. I was not frightened while hanging on to the shears. We were so intent on getting our jobs done that nothing else mattered. Finally the resistance cards were in place. The radar worked again.

The food that was loaded from the base in Perth was not withstanding. The eggs were rotten after the first few days at sea. The cooks reverted to the gummy and tasteless powered variety. The butter was rancid. There was very little beef. The mutton was only fair. Much of it was from older sheep, and the smell was stronger than the taste. We had ram instead of lamb. All the poultry was "New York Cut." The guts were still intact, and the internal organs were removed after the chicken or turkey was thawed.

Most of the poultry was improperly packed. Many of the wings' edges and smaller pieces were seriously damaged by freezer burn. The cooks and the captain had a running battle about the quality of the food sent to the wardroom. The new, black steward's mate, Bennie Wilson, was in the middle of the conflict. He shuttled between the galley and the wardroom with food and instructions.

On February 26, we were back in the same stop along the beach. Less than a week had passed since our narrow escape in the shallow water off Padaran Point. The Japanese air coverage was intense. Radar-equipped planes kept us jumping day and night. It was almost like we were in the middle of a disturbed hive of bees. The USS *Blenny* and USS *Becuna* each sunk a ship during the previous night. Our station was between the two burning hulls. Only small sailboats were visible from our submerged position.

When we were ready to surface at dusk, depth charges started to fall. Fourteen charges explored near us, but they didn't cause any damage. After it was dark, the captain took the risk and surfaced to charge a battery. During the night we dove several times to escape low-flying Japanese planes. A couple of times the *Guavina* lived up to her name and slid along the muddy bottom.

The Japanese charts were better than nothing. They didn't show all we needed to know about the water along the coast. According to a report from Naval Intelligence, the strongest anti-submarine force in the whole empire protected Cam Ranh Bay. The hunter-killer groups consisted of destroyers, sound boats, and other auxiliary units.

At 0300, Japanese surveillance planes forced us down. Although the captain checked frequently with the periscope and SD radar, we were kept down for nearly twenty hours. Air became very stale and low on oxygen. About 2100, the word passed that the smoking lamp was out. To get a final charge of nicotine, men with the habit puffed desperately. The cigarettes gave off a foul-smelling, dark brown smoke that almost choked us nonsmokers. Most of the crew stretched out on the deck and were very quiet. I was on and off the JP sound gear as our underwater stay progressed, which helped beak the tension and monotony. During our long stay underwater, the captain moved us toward the open seas. With morning approaching, it was possible to get a little breath of air and enough surface time to charge the batteries.

The next night we moved back toward the beach. Our detectors keyed in on a steady contact from the electronic surveillance station on the beach. The captain decided to dive at 2300 hours. When we tried to surface at 0730, the depth chargers started failing. After a half dozen dropped, we rigged for silent running, where we eased out to open sea. The pressure of the anti-sub force was intense. All of us were very restless and uncomfortable.

Resurfacing at about 1300 hours, our radioman received a message. We were to proceed toward a specific location on a secret mission. It took a full day before we arrived at the designated place. The following day was spent underwater waiting for some type of vessel to pass. One of the officers dropped a hint that we were waiting for a German U-Boat. Apparently Navy Intelligence had decoded information about the projected course of the submarine, but it had changed and we didn't see it.

That evening a message came for us to proceed to Subic Bay for refit. Subic was not where we wanted to go, but it was better than staying in the war zone. Our instructions were to proceed along a recognized safety lane through the South China Sea to the

Philippines. Very few Japanese planes were flying on that side of the South China Sea, and the American planes knew the location of the safety lane. Our vigilance relaxed a little as we moved at a good speed where we felt fairly secure.

It was always cleaning time the last day or two out of port. Men not on watch cleaned the bulkheads, mopped floors, and polished the equipment. Everyone was busy, yet there was a feeling of anticipation as we were only a few hours from Subic Bay. We had plenty of fuel and we were moving along on three engines. The fourth engine was putting an equalization charge on the batteries, to have them ready for our stay in port. The SD radar picked up a plane at twenty miles, and the bridge identified it as a U.S. PBM [patrol bomb] flying boat.

The plane would not answer the IFF identification query and ignored our attempt to contact it with a blinker light. When the plane was about a mile away, we could see the bomb door open. This was not the time to push for further identification. In seconds, the men dropped down the hatch. We crash-dived at a 14 percent angle. A bomb exploded close as we came to a zero bubble at 350 feet. The whole boat shuddered. We were lucky, no damage this time. Some of the lookouts who had called it a PBM began to wonder if they had made the correct identification.

After a short wait under the water, we surfaced to send an urgent radio message. After giving our location in the safety zone, the captain complained to headquarters that an American plane had bombed us. Some of the officers promised to go to the Army base and get the guy. Suddenly we hated Army flyboys.

Late that afternoon a spontaneous combustion fire broke out in a pile of greasy rags in the after engine room. The smoke filled the entire boat, but there was no damage. Increased ventilation soon cleared the smoke.

This was the worst run any of the crew had experienced. The entire run was filled with crisis and excitement. It started with a hot-run torpedo out of Exmouth Bay in the Indian Ocean. A day before arriving at Subic Bay, we were bombed by an American plane. The thought of asking to be transferred to the relief crew entered my mind. The thought of spending the rest of the war in Subic Bay was worse than going back to sea.

In March 1945, we approached the Philippine Island of Luzon. The SJ radar picked up the high mountainous slopes when we were fifty miles at sea. As we moved closer, I hoped the American Army and Navy ships had conquered the Japanese on this part of the island. At Subic Bay we were forty miles north of Manila. It felt great to have my feet on solid ground.

* * *

As of 2007, Marion L. Shinn RT2/c was a member and the Commander of the Idaho Submarine Veterans of World War II, the National Officer of Nominating Chairman and the Resolutions Chairman, a member of the United States Submarine Veterans Inc., and a Holland Club Member of the Hawkbill Base of Southern Idaho.

USS *Tinosa* (SS-283)

USS *Tinosa* (SS-283) was a *Gato*-class submarine. She was commissioned on January 15, 1943. She completed twelve war patrols and sunk sixteen enemy ships totaling 64,655 tons.

Information taken from https://en.wikipedia.org/wiki/USS _Tinosa_(SS-283)

LOYAL A. HUSON

From information submitted by Loyal A. Huson to Mary Nida Smith

At seventeen, Loyal A. Huson joined the U.S. Navy in Chicago, Illinois. On June 11, 1943, he entered boot camp and then a sixteen-week torpedo school at Great Lakes Naval Training Center, after which he reported to San Diego Naval Submarine Base for advanced torpedo, electric torpedo, and submarine schools.

After torpedo school, Huson was sent to US SUB-PAC, Pearl Harbor, December 1944, where he was assigned to Submarine Relief Crew 45. Later, on February 17, 1945, he reported for duty aboard the USS *Tinosa* (SS-283), a *Gato*-class 1,500-ton fleet type submarine and the first ship of the United States Navy named for a poisonous, black tropical fish. Huson's quarters were in the After Torpedo Room during "Battle Stations

USS *Tinosa* (SS-283), Loyal A. Huson. Photo from the archives of Loyal A. Huson.

Submerged." For "Battle Stations Surface," he manned a 50-cal. machine gun. At both stations, he was involved in enemy combat.

Lt. Commander R.C. Latham was the commander during the time Huson served as Torpedoman's Mate, during *Tinosa*'s ninth, tenth, eleventh, and twelfth patrols.

* * *

On March 17, 1945, the *Tinosa* sailed on her ninth war patrol from the Marshall Islands to the East China Sea, her mission to continue testing the mine-detecting capabilities of her temperamental FM sonar, while also observing Japanese shipping operations and taking reconnaissance photographs. This patrol ended early on April 7 at Apra Harbor, Guam, because of recurring unexplainable damage to her bow plane rigging gear.

While undergoing repairs at Guam, the *Tinosa* was installed with new FM sonar mine detection equipment, which greatly improved her sonar range and the collection of data on their way

USS *Tinosa* (SS-283), Loyal A. Huson. Photo from the archives of Loyal A. Huson.

to the Truck Islands (tenth war patrol, which commenced on April 28). On May 7, near Moen Island, she narrowly escaped damage from bombs dropped by enemy airplanes. The *Tinosa* bombarded a Japanese installation on Ulul Island the night of May 14 and was able to provide numerous photographs for intelligence officers when the boat arrived back at Guam on May 16.

On May 29, 1945, on the twelfth war patrol, *Tinosa* was under way to the Sea of Japan as a newly formed "wolf pack" of nine submarines called "Hydeman's Hellcats." This special group was selected for the extremely dangerous mission of disrupting Japanese shipping operations inside the sea of Japan. The Hellcats were comprised of Commander Earl T. Hydeman's "HepCats" (USS *Sea Dog*, USS *Crevelle*, and USS *Spadefish*), Commander George E. Pierce's "Pole Cats" (USS *Tunny*, USS *Skate*, and USS *Bonefish*), and Commander Robert D. Risser's "Bobcats" (USS *Flying Fish*, USS *Bowfish*, and USS *Tinosa*).

The mission was code-named "Operation Barney," after Commander William Bernard "Barney" Sieglaff, the man Vice Admiral Charles A. Lockwood chose to take over training, planning, and execution of the mission. It would be Sieglaff's responsibility to insert this pack of submarines capable of using the new FM sonar into the Sea of Japan through the heavily mined Tsushima Strait at its southern end, and ensure that any submarine returning there in the future could accurately plot the location of those minefields.

USS *Tinosa* (SS-283)

En route to the Sea of Japan, on June 2, the *Tinosa* rescued ten survivors of a ditched B-29, who were transferred to the USS *Scabbard Fish* (SS-397) two days later.

Beginning on June 4, Hydeman's Hellcats stealthily threaded their way through the minefields in the Tsushima Strait and into the Sea of Japan—three subs at a time, over a three-day period,

143

USS *Tinosa* (SS-283)

with the *Tinosa* making its entry on June 6—for an offensive patrol off the west-central Japanese coast of Honshu. Working in packs of three, the submarines began their attacks at sunset on June 9, to sink any type of Japanese shipping vessels they encountered. The *Tinosa*'s first target was a 2,300-ton vessel, heavily loaded, which it torpedoed that same evening.

On June 12, *Tinosa* waged a bold daytime surface gun battle against the *Keit Maru*, a Japanese sea truck, sinking it in short order. In all, the *Tinosa* sank four Japanese ships (two on June 20) and damaged a fifth before their patrol ended.

At sunset on June 23, eight of the nine Hellcat's submarines gathered at a rendezvous point near the northern end of the Sea of Japan. The *Bonefish* (SS-223) failed to appear, and while there was not much concern about it at the time, it was later presumed, and then officially declared, that she perished with all eighty-five hands on board while on war patrol in enemy waters, on or after June 18, 1945.

About midnight on June 24, in dense fog, the eight remaining subs made a daring high-speed escape out of the Sea of Japan through the narrow, heavily patrolled La Perouse Strait. The *Tinosa* then sailed for Midway Island, where it docked on June 30, only long enough to refuel.

On July 4, 1945, with colors flying, the USS *Tinosa* successfully ended its eleventh war patrol by arriving safely at Pearl Harbor.

USS *Tinosa* (SS-283) crew, 1945

After a twenty-one-day refit and another two weeks of testing and training exercises, the *Tinosa* started their thirteenth war patrol on August 13, 1945. This patrol was abruptly terminated on August 15 by Japan's unconditional surrender to the Allied Forces following the bombings of Hiroshima and Nagasaki.

* * *

Each crew member received a scroll certificate, with which Submarine Force Pacific Fleet "extends to Loyal A. Huson membership in the distinguished order of Mighty Mine Dodgers, a small band of brave men of high courage who have completed with skill, ingenuity, and tenacity a task that required transit of the most dangerous of war waters, through enemy minefields and penetrating what the Emperor of Japan considered his inviolate of war waters—the

USS *Tinosa* (SS-283), Pearl Harbor, 1945, photo from the archives of Loyal A. Huson

Sea of Japan. No weapon of Dai Nippon could halt these determined men. They did willfully and with due knowledge of dangers involved, carry out their assigned task to emerge with incontrovertible proof of the success of their daring, thus becoming members of the Mighty Mine Dodgers and entitled to all rights and privileges thereof. Let all men who read this scroll be forever grateful and respectful of these heroic American submariners who went in and especially to those who gave their lives in this operation. The job was superlatively 'well done.'" —Signed, Charles A. Lockwood, Vice Admiral USN Awarded: Submarine Combat Insignia with three stars, Asiatic-Pacific with Bronze Star, American Theater, and Victory and Good Conduct medals.

* * *

U.S.S. TINOSA (SS283)
Care of Fleet Postoffice,
San Francisco, California

22 January 1946

From: The Commanding Officer, U.S.S. TINOSA.
To :   **Loyal A. HUSON**

      This note is just an informal tribute from the skipper to his officers and crew. It is written to express appreciation for the part you played in making the " MIGHTY T" the ship she was.
      The enclosed MIGHTY MINE DODGER certificates and cards reflect the personal interest and pride of Admiral Lockwood, Commander Submarines, Pacific Fleet. They are forwarded to you by me with great happiness in memory of a superb fighting unit, welded together into a happy team by our mutual trust, confidence, and joy achieved by working wholeheartedly together on a worthwhile job.
      Whereever you go and whatever you do, thanks, good luck, and best personal regards,

R C Latham

R.C. LATHAM

USS *Tinosa* (SS-283). Mighty Mine Dodgers Certificate Letter from Commanding Officer R. C. Latham to Loyal A. Huson. From the archives of Loyal A. Huson.

USS *Tinosa* (SS-283) Mighty Mine Dodgers Certificate. From the archives of Loyal A. Huson.

Two books were written and a movie produced about "Operation Barney": *Hellcats: The Epic Story of World War II's Most Daring Submarine Raid* by Peter Sasgen and *Hellcats of the Sea* by Charles A. Lockwood and Hans Christian Adamson. The movie was *Hellcats of the Navy* with Ronald Reagan and Nancy Davis (later Mrs. Reagan).

* * *

USS *Tinosa* (SS-283) *Hellcats* book cover

USS *Tinosa* (SS-283) Hellcats U.S. Navy poster

Loyal Huson, TM3/c 1944-1945, USS *Tinosa* (SS-283) is a member of the USSVI Twin Lakes Base, Mountain Home.

USS *Torsk* (SS-423)

USS *Torsk* (SS-423) is one of two *Tench*-class submarines still located inside the United States. Nicknamed the "Galloping Ghost of the Japanese Coast," *Torsk* made two war patrols off Japan in 1945, sinking one cargo vessel and two coastal defense frigates. The latter of these, torpedoed on August 14, 1945, was the last enemy ship sunk by the U.S. Navy in World War II.

Information taken from https://en.wikipedia.org/wiki/USS _Torsk_(SS-423)

ERVIN O. SCHMIDT
From information submitted by Ervin O. Schmidit to Mary Nida Smith

Ervin O. Schmidt, RM1/C (SS) USN-RET, from the state of Washington, joined the Navy at a young age, as did most the men of that era. Schmidt and his family emigrated from Germany in 1923 when he was seven years old. He grew up in Wisconsin on a farm. While still in his youth, he went to work for the Civilian Conservation Corp in the late 1930s. In 1940, he joined the Navy.

Schmidt was aboard the USS *California* moored at Pearl Harbor on December 7, 1941. The aerial attack launched by the Japanese caused the ship enormous damage. Ninety-eight crew members were lost and sixty-one wounded. Schmidt was pulled from the water by a motorized launch. In the confusion, he was listed as missing in action. Before his family learned differently, they had held a funeral in his honor.

Schmidt was a crew member on the USS *Saury* (SS-189) during five war patrols. The *Saury* earned seven battle stars during World War II.

On December 31, 1944, the USS *Torsk* went to sea for the first time and did only two war patrols before being assigned to the Submarine Squadron 8 as part of the Submarine School in new London, Connecticut, for a training vessel.

Ervin O. Schmidt's first war patrol on the USS *Torsk* occurred in April 1945. Its crew was assigned to serve as the lifeguard for B-29s while they made raids over the Japanese Empire. Later they operated off Kii Stuido and Honshu. During the first part of the war, so many ships had been sunk that it left very little for them to attack.

On May 30, 1945, the USS *Balao* (SS-205) had dodged four torpedoes while being fired upon by a Japanese submarine. "I intercepted the message it sent to COMSUBPAC," said Schmidt. "We had to transfer 3/c E. D. Wolfe to the *Balao* on May 29, 1945, in a rubber boat, for he had a painful appendicitis attack. Robert Flaridy almost had his foot smashed while rotating the torpedoes in the forward torpedo room before the attack.

"On June 5, 1945, we left the patrol area of the Sea of Japan for Midway, Honolulu, and the Royal Hawaiian Hotel, for two weeks of R&R." They later sailed to Guam.

On July 15, 1945, the submarine was sent on their second war patrol to the Sea of Japan. They rescued seven Japanese seamen after their ship had been sunk by a U.S. plane. In Tokyo, the *Torsk* was maneuvering to fire her rear torpedoes to sink an enemy tanker, but it missed. It hit a railroad bridge that had a train crossing filled with ammunition. The sky lit up as the loud booming sounds continued, as if it had hit several large enemy tankers.

They continued to confront the enemy in combat action. They sunk two small ships. This action earned *Torsk* the distinction of firing the last torpedo while sinking the last Japanese ships of World War II. The following day, August 15, 1945, the "cease fire" was ordered to all U.S. forces.

As stated in the tribute by Joseph P. Kennedy II, Massachusetts House of Representatives, on Thursday, November 14, 1991, Schmidt met and married his wife during the war. When the war was over, he returned home to the Pacific Northwest, where he and his wife raised four children. Despite financial hardships, the family went skiing in the winter on skis that cost fifty cents, purchased from the Salvation Army Thrift Store, and they went camping every summer. They remained active in the Boy Scouts of America for decades. One son became an Eagle Scout and went on to graduate from Harvard.

Several USS *Torsk* battle flags were painted during August and September 1945. Schmidt painted one with oil on a navy canvas. On September 3, 1944, they left the Sea of Japan to return to the States. "My flag was donated to the USS *Torsk* Museum on October 22, 1994, at the fiftieth Christening ceremony, by me and Patricia Schmoke, wife of Baltimore's mayor. What a special day this was for all the *Torsk* plank owners who were there for this great day," recalled Schmidt.

* * *

As of this writing, Ervin O. Schmidt RM1/C, a Pearl Harbor Survivor, had been the U.S. Submarine Veterans WWII Commander for two years for the Lockwood Chapter, and he was the Washington State Commander (2005). He was an active member of the Lockwood Chapter USSVI, Chaplain and plank owner of the Seattle Base, USSVI. In the summer of 2005, he was to travel to Washington, DC, to visit the Memorial of the *Torsk*. In 2013, Schmidt served as the Grand Marshal for the Independence Day parade in the city of Edmonds, Washington. He was ninety-seven.[6]

---

[6] http://www.heraldnet.com/article/20130704/NEWS01/707049907

USS *Pogy* (SS-266)

USS *Pogy* (SS-266) was a *Gato*-class submarine. She was commissioned January 10, 1943. *Pogy* sank sixteen ships totaling 62,633 tons, and received eight battle stars for her World War II service.

Information taken from https://en.wikipedia.org/wiki/USS _Pogy_(SS-266)

War Patrols

On April 7, 1944, *Pogy* departed on her sixth patrol, southeast of Japan. Two weeks later, on the night of April 28, she sighted and sank a Japanese submarine (I-183). She then attacked and sank a freighter on May 5 and a medium freight on May 15. Three days later, she sank a 20-ton sampan by gunfire, and took five of her crew prisoner. On May 20, *Pogy* destroyed a small trawler and arrived back in Pearl Harbor on May 29. She departed Pearl Harbor on June 1 for a West Coast Navy yard, arriving at Hunter's Point, San Francisco, California, on June 8. On June 20, Lieutenant Commander P. G. Molteni Jr., USN, relieved Lieutenant Commander Metcalf as commanding officer.

Pogy departed for Pearl Harbor on September 17, 1944, after a complete overhaul. After a training period, she got under way on October 13 for the seventh war patrol in the Nasei Shoto and water south of Japan, but made no contacts before returning to Midway on December 2.

On December 27, *Pogy* sailed on her eighth patrol for islands of the Nampo Shoto (Bonin and Volcano). On January 14, 1945, she made an unsuccessful torpedo attack on a convoy of three freighters. No other opportunity to attack presented itself during the patrol, and the ship returned to Midway on February 11, 1945.

On February 22, Lieutenant Commander J. M. Bowers, USN, relieved Lieutenant Commander P. G. Molteni Jr., as commanding officer.

On March 12, 1945, *Pogy* got under way for her ninth patrol from Midway in the area south of Tokyo Bay. The patrol spanned sixty-four days, of which thirty-one days were spent in the area.

April 1, Japanese hated U.S. Submarines. Sampans appeared to look like they were filled with the enemy. They opened fire with the 40mm and then the machine gun. Fourteen rounds were fired. Then they quickly got out of there, for they could not afford to take any more hits. *Pogy* was beat up pretty bad. They had to beat lead plugs into the holes so they could dive, but it continued to slowly leak.

On April 29, 1945, at 1302 hours, *Pogy* sighted a B-29 and a PBY circling low over the water. She made radio contact with them and was informed there were numerous life rafts in the water. *Pogy* closed in on them and made ready to begin receiving downed aviation personnel. Over the next several hours, she took aboard ten survivors from USAAF B-29 number 840. The survivors said one crewman was missing because his parachute failed to open. On May 5, *Pogy* transferred the aviators to the USS *Orion* at Saipan.

On May 6, she departed for Pearl Harbor, arriving on May 15 for refit.

On July 2, *Pogy* departed Pearl Harbor for the Sea of Japan on her tenth and last war patrol. She made a run under the minefields and patrolled in the "Emperor's private ocean" until V-J [Victory or Japan] day. Hunting was better on this patrol.

* * *

Pogy was placed out of commission in the U.S. Atlantic Reserve Fleet on July 20, 1946, at New London, Connecticut. She was struck from the Navy List on September 1, 1958, and sold May 1, 1959.

Pogy received eight Battle Stars on the Asiatic Pacific Area Service Medal. DeVore made the last four war patrols on the USS *Pogy*.

ROBERT L. DEVORE SR.

"I Went on Strike in the Navy"

Written by Robert L. DeVore Sr.

Reprinted from *Polaris* / June 2012

I may have been the first man to go on strike in the Navy and get away with it. My boat, *Pogy*, didn't return to the States until October 1945. I was a Torpedoman Third Class but had taken the test for Second Class during our long journey home and was promised the rating. When we tied up at the State Pier in New London, all hands went to work on the boat; cleaning, repairing, etc. I was miffed because I was denied the rating. I went topside and sat on the capstan from morning until noon. The executive officer (XO) inquired of the chief of the boat (COB) why I was not working. When the XO heard the story, he immediately asked the gunnery

Robert L. DeVore,
Torpedoman First Class
Submarine Pogy (SS-266

USS *Pogy* (SS-266), Robert L. DeVore. Photo from the archives of Robert L. DeVore Sr.

officer if this was true. The gunnery officer said yes, it was true. The XO ordered that I be rated second class. I was a happy camper after that.

* * *

DeVore was assigned to the USS *Pogy* at Mare Island, California. On board he had several duties, including cooking and serving food. While he was acting as "laundry queen," the washing machine broke down. If they were lucky, the crew received a change of clothes once a week and the laundry had to be done in a bucket until the machine was repaired. —from *Experiencing War: Stories from the Veterans History Project,* The Library of Congress, American Folklife Center, October 26, 2011.

"Mascot on *Pogy* (SS-226)"

Written by Robert L. DeVore Sr.

Reprinted from *Polaris* / June 2014

A young pup followed a sailor on board the *Pogy* in Pearl Harbor in June 1945. The crew decided to keep the pup and name him "Pogy Pete," and the forward torpedo room would be his home for the boat's tenth war patrol in the Sea of Japan. When Captain Bowes saw the pup, he immediately claimed him for his own and instructed the torpedomen to care for him. He ate galley food and was potty trained. He was a playful pooch and the crew would often come to the torpedo room to pet the pup for good luck. He was restricted to the forward room, not being able to get over the hatch combing going into the forward battery compartment. One day he chewed on a piece of soap and began to froth at the mouth. A torpedoman set the pup into officer's quarters and yelled, "Mad dog!" It cleared the officer's quarters. The torpedoman got a good chewing-out.

After going through the "dummy minefield" in Guam, Pogy Pete got a short shore leave and then back on board, shoved off for the Sea of Japan.

He did well while going through the minefields for about ten hours submerged, except his ears would perk up when a mine cable scraped along the cable barriers. He, along with the crew, was relieved when the boat surfaced the night of July 25 and they could breathe fresh air once more.

Pogy Pete was there when *Pogy* sunk a 7,000-ton Japanese merchant ship. He didn't like the explosions of the torpedoes neither when the boilers blew up on the boat when cold water hit the hot boilers, nor when the depth charges began exploding around the sub. His favorite foxhole was squeezing under the lower bunk.

On July 31, sleepy-eyed Pete was there once again when *Pogy* went to battle stations at 0300 on a 10,000-ton Japanese ship. The boat was unable to get a shot off before depth charges began raining down on the sub. Once again, Pete ran under a lower bunk to escape the explosions.

Pete was never able to get accustomed to the explosions, when once more the boat hit another 10,000-ton oil tanker and like before, depth charges exploded all around the submarine on August 1.

Pogy Pete was getting really stressed out when a 5,000-ton oil tanker was sunk on August 5. It was becoming obvious that Pete would rather be anyplace rather than on a submarine in time of war. His hair was getting thin from bunk springs on the lower bunk.

The submarine *Pogy* was in 210 feet of water when she fired on a yard oiler. The oiler didn't draw enough water for a hit, but the torpedoes went under the ship and hit rocks on shore and exploded. These last explosions may have been all Pete could take.

On August 11, the boat was preparing to leave the Sea of Japan, but the American surface craft had the Japanese bottled in the north and didn't want the sub to interfere and depart just yet.

August 12, a sad day for the crew. Pogy Pete became deathly ill and passed away. That night he was buried with honors in the Sea of Japan. He well-earned the Submarine Combat Pin and all the campaign ribbons for that patrol. Hawaii should be proud that one of its own gave his life while defending his country.

Many submarine crews carried mascots on board their boats, and many lost their lives when the submarine was lost.

"Last Patrol and Return of *Pogy*"

Written by Robert L. DeVore Sr.

Reprinted from *Polaris* / September 2011

Pogy entered the minefields submerged early on July 25, 1945. The purpose was to get into the Sea of Japan and sink ships. After a ten-hour run, *Pogy* was on the surface by 2031 hours the same day. The boat met up with two Japanese men and a woman huddled together on what appeared to be part of a ship's deck. One of the crewmen attempted to communicate with the survivors, but to no avail. Captain Bowers checked the wind and stated they were being blown out to sea. Therefore no action was taken to destroy them or bring them on board.

A short time later, five pips showed up on the radar dead ahead. They were sub chasers bearing down on the *Pogy*. The boat found a cove and settled on the bottom to avoid being detected. The sub that was close behind *Pogy* caught hell all night long from depth charge attacks.

Early in the morning, *Pogy* came up to periscope depth and proceeded patrolling the sea, firing its acoustic, electrical, and steam-type torpedoes into enemy ships. On one occasion, the captain lined up on a large target when the XO on the search periscope called to the captain that he saw blonde hair flying in the breeze on the target ship. It was a Russian ship and the attack was called off.

The sub had to remain in the sea longer than expected, because U.S. warships had the Japanese ships "bottled up" in the area where *Pogy* was to exit the sea. At one point it was thought that they might have to be interned by the Russians because our fuel and food were running low. No one wanted that to happen, so the speaker made a dash of 21.5 knots through the northern straits exiting the sea. On August 15 at midnight, *Pogy* was running on the surface in the Sea of Okhotsk, heading for Midway Island using the 12-cylinder auxiliary engine to save fuel.

We received news that the war had ended. Each crew member was given a shot of whiskey to celebrate the occasion. Sailors came topside to sunbathe. Speaker wires were strung through the hatch for music topside. Then came a message saying to be careful, for some of the enemy had not received the word of the war's end.

At Midway, *Pogy* had to take on fuel before a battery charge could be started. Food was brought on board to supplement the beans and rice the crew had been eating for days. Some personnel came aboard for traveling to Pearl Harbor.

At Pearl Harbor, *Pogy* took on a load of torpedoes to carry to the United States, and more personnel came on board.

While running up the east coast off Cape Hatteras near North Carolina, the boat ran into a terrible storm of up to ninety-knot winds. Water was whipping through the periscope shears, soaking everyone on the bridge. The boat was rolling at dangerous degrees. A torpedo cradle strap parted, allowing the 3,000-pound torpedo and cradle to bang against its stops, bending the stop-pins before a new strap could be put in place.

It was difficult knowing just where we were and the speed we were making against the storm. The skipper sent the quartermaster topside to get a bearing on anything in the sky to pinpoint our location and speed. The quartermaster came from topside and reported according to his calculation the ship was backing down three knots, and where we were, he didn't know.

The skipper dove the boat to 100 feet to try and escape the storm and for the cook to prepare a hot meal for the crew. Everything was going fine, and the cook had hot soup on the galley range. Then a ground swell began to lift us to the surface and nothing could stop the upward movement. Pots and pans went in every direction. The cook was using words meant only for sailor's ears to describe his predicament. We tried going down once more, but the boat would not remain submerged. We rode out the storm for several days before a calm came at last and we had hot food again.

We pulled into Staten Island, New York, in October 1945, and it was cold. We had no winter clothing, but winter clothing was supplied so sailors could go ashore. Some of the crew had enough points to be discharged from service while there.

With its battle flags displayed high on the conning tower, the boat, needing repairing and a paint job, moved to New Bedford, Massachusetts, for Navy Day [October 27]. The mayor gave the crew the "keys to the city" and the liberty was great.

Pogy had a good record of sinking enemy ships. She was the tenth of the top ten with the most enemy tonnage sunk during her ten war patrols. Captains Whales, Metcalf, and Bowers all received Navy Crosses for a job well done. The crew earned Silver, Bronze, and Battle Stars.

"Submarine Battle Fears"
Written by Robert L. DeVore Sr.
Reprinted from *Polaris* / September 2014

Battle causing fear is probably the worst kind of fear. I know it is, for submarine men. Fear causes grown men to cry, tremble, and pale. It has happened during heavy depth-charge and depth-bomb attacks. I saw it happen when our sub ran aground in a terrible storm, and once when rammed by a surface craft, losing 40,000 gallons of fuel oil.

My most memorable event was told to me by a shipmate, "Cannonball" Hammond, a torpedoman's mate 2/c from Iowa. Cannonball had gone topside to relieve a lookout to get some fresh air. While on lifeguard duty, picking up downed pilots, a B-24 Liberator came in and began circling, signaling with his IFF. We were unable to respond, and on his third circle he opened his bomb bay doors and strafed and dropped his bomb, missing but very close. I had an electric torpedo pulled halfway out of the tube, checking the voltage and electrolyte. The handhold plate flew from my hand, and I never did find it later.

The OOD yelled to clear the bridge and to "Dive, dive!" Coming down, Cannonball hit the control room deck so hard it jarred his ankle up to his hip bone.

The attack was brutal, knocking out all communication topside, putting 50-cal. bullet holes in the periscope shears and the radio cable housing, and pouring salt water onto the TBL in the radio shack. Upon surfacing that night, lead was pounded into the bullet holes to stop the leaks. Gunner checked the ready ammunition lockers topside and found one four-inch ammunition locker flooded by bullet holes. The shells had missed the ammunition by inches. The last bullet hole found was through the horn.

Later, Cannonball Hammond asked the doc if he had any cyanide pills to pass out if people were trapped in a compartment and began to suffocate for lack of air. The doc said no, he did not have such pills. Cannonball asked the doc what he would do if trapped in a compartment. Doc pulled a .45-cal. pistol from his belt under his shirt and said, "I'd use this!"

I noticed Cannonball's limp when I picked him up at the bus station. He said clearing the bridge that fearful day caused the limp, and it had gotten worse down through the years. He never turned the injury in at the veteran's hospital or asked for any compensation for his war wound. He was very proud to have served his country.

When he was at my home, he set his deceased wife's picture on the dresser at the foot of his bed. This gave him comfort, for he loved her very much. He never wanted to worry her with his injury, he said.

Many sub sailors had bad dreams after the war. I know I did.

Information compiled by Mary Nida Smith[7, 8]

Robert L. DeVore was born March 3, 1926, in Metcalf County, Kentucky, and divided his time as a youngster between city life and on a farm. After his dad died in 1940, he continued school until his seventeenth birthday in 1943, when he decided to drop out and enlist in the Navy. He attended boot camp at Great Lakes, Illinois, and when he was finished he was chosen to attend torpedoman's school. During torpedo school he had a difficult time understanding, until his commanding officer ordered him to teach a class in exploder mechanisms, which helped him. From there, he volunteered for submarine school and trained on an older boat with controls that were hard to operate. He had failed the seaman first class test three times, so he was only ranked second class.

Besides the USS *Pogy*, DeVore served on the USS *Grouper* (SS-214) from 1947–1950, and the USS *Bugara* (SS-331) and USS *Caiman* (SS-323) during the Korean War. He graduated from Instructor's School at San Diego and instructor Submarine Reserves at Cleveland, Ohio, on USS *Gar* (SS-206) from

---

[7] *Pogy*, the Veterans History Project, The Library of Congress, American Folklife Center

[8] *U.S. Submarine Veterans of World War II*, Volume Three (Taylor Publishing Company)

1953–1956, and later he served as chief of the boat and driving officer on USS *Hardhead* (SS-365) in the Atlantic.

DeVore graduated from Recruiter's School at Bainbridge in 1962, and was assigned Recruiter Duty in Louisville, Kentucky. He helped organize FRA and SubVets World War II Chapters in Louisville, and retired in June 1966. He was a supervisor with USDA, an ordained Baptist minister, and is married to the former Rosemary Reddy of Cleveland. They have five sons and two daughters. DeVore is the editor of the *Polaris* (WWII magazine).

USS *Tunny* (SS/SSG/APSS/LPSS-282)

USS *Tunny* (SS/SSG/APSS/LPSS-282) was a *Gato*-class submarine which served in World War II and the Vietnam War. She was commissioned on September 1, 1942. USS *Tunny* received nine battle stars and two Presidential Unit Citations for her World War II service, and five battle stars for her operations during the Vietnam War.

Information taken from https://en.wikipedia.org/wiki/USS _Tunny_(SS-282)

Written by Marvin S. Blair

Stealth Beneath the Sea: The Wet Cold War by David Colley

I was born June 8, 1924, in Killeen, Texas, and raised in Houston, Texas. I received my commission as an ensign in the Navy in 1944.

I went to sea on USS *Tunny* in April 1955, and one dark night ran out on the deck with the launch crew and armed and fused the first nuclear weapon (non-nuclear yield) ever launched by a submarine. I still have the warhead safing plugs out of that weapon.

When I was the commanding officer (CO) in 1958, CINC-PACFLT (Commander In Chief, U.S. Pacific Fleet) asked us to fire a Regulus I with a thermonuclear warhead in its nose as part of the Fleet's firepower demonstration off Okinawa for the SEATO (Southeast Asian Treaty Organization) Nations top brass. For one plus unbelievable hours, I was designated formation guide for Task Force 77 (two or three aircraft carriers, two heavy cruisers, and about eleven or so frigates and destroyers). That may be a "first" for a submarine, too! We had an aircraft carrier about 500 yards away on our star bow, another one about 500 yards on our star quarter, the third one astern of those two, and so forth. What was impressive to me was that the first four ships in the column were flying four-star American admiral's flags!

Needless to say, the operation was flawless. We submerged, then battle-surfaced, ran out and started the missile, armed the warhead, and away it went. We set the altitude controller to fly at 3,000 feet so the SEATO people could see it. We guided it out about seventy miles, turned it around, and flew it down the entire starboard side of Task Force 77! Then we took it out about seventy miles, turned it around and guided it so the warhead (non-nuclear yield) would detonate about 3,000 yards on our port beam.

USS *Tunny* (SSG-282)

Man, I've never felt such a blast! It almost blew me off the bridge. I was told later that the thing that absolutely blew their minds was the fact that, as they watched the missile launch in a huge cloud of smoke from its booster rockets (which of course completely blanked out the *Tunny* from view), then looked back at where *Tunny* was, guess what? *Tunny* was completely submerged and out of sight except for one periscope and our guidance radar. We got a month's liberty in WestPac from CINCPACFLT for that performance. I have the safing plug from that shot, too.

Then, either the night before or two nights before entering Pearl Harbor from this trip to WestPac, I got a flash message from COM-SUBPAC (Commander, Submarine Force U.S. Pacific Fleet), telling me that the Marines had landed in Lebanon, and the whole military establishment had gone to DEFCON (DEFense CONdition) 2! I was told to maintain radar silence, run darkened ship, and commence zigzagging. Also, to enter port no matter the time, proceed to West Loch, and load two Regulus I missiles with thermonuclear warheads. After that, proceed to the SubBase and load with fuel and stores, and *be ready to deploy in no more than thirty-six hours!*

What shocked me the most was the order to enter port no matter what time. In Pearl, *no one* moved in the harbor after sunset or before sunrise. We actually deployed in thirty-two hours. When my executive officer got home, his family came down to the dock. I was only home for two hours, and one section didn't get liberty at all.

When we deployed, this turned out to be the first deterrent missile patrol ever made. The rest of the Regulus I boats didn't start making those patrols for more than a year.

About forty years later, the *Tunny* and its crew were recognized for this pioneering patrol by being awarded the Polaris Deterrent Patrol Pin.

I was selected for nuclear power training in 1959 and, as far as I know, I was the first officer selected that didn't have a college degree, although I did have three years of college.

I put the *Robert E. Lee* (the third Polaris sub) in commission as XO of the Gold Crew, and made two deterrent missile patrols on her while operating out of the Holy Loch, Scotland. I was then ordered back for Polaris A-3 training, attended schools at Dam Neck Naval Base again, attended Westinghouse Bettis School of Reactor Engineering, spent three months in Admiral Rickover's office, was approved by the congressional committee on atomic energy (or something like that) to command a nuclear powered submarine, and reported to the *Daniel Webster*, putting her in commission as CO Blue Crew. We deployed on patrol with the first load of Polaris A-3 missiles. The A-3 was a 2,500–2,600 mile solid grain rocket with three thermonuclear warheads. I made four deterrent missile patrols on her, three while operating out of Rota, Spain, and the fourth from the Holy Loch, Scotland.

Understand that each of those Polaris deterrent missile patrols was seventy-five days submerged! One of the great thrills that I had was being promoted to captain while on our fourth patrol. I think I may have been one of the first that this happened to on sub.

I was asked for by RADM (Rear Admiral) Gene Fluckey to come to Pearl Harbor and take command of the Polaris Training Facility there for two years. Then, three years on COMSUBPAC's staff as Assistant Chief of Staff for Logistics (N4), followed by one and a half years at SAC Headquarters, where I was Deputy Commander of the National Strategies Target List Division, Deputy to an Air Force General and Polaris submarine advisor to the Commander and Chief of the Strategic Air Command.

I made thirteen war patrols on five different submarines during the Cold War.

I retired the last day of 1972, and my name was placed on the Retired List as of January 1, 1973. So endeth my long take of twenty-eight years as an officer in submarines.

[This information was provided by Captain Marvin S. Blair to Carl Schmidt in the book *Stealth Beneath the Sea: The "Wet Cold War"* by David Colley.]

* * *

Captain Marvin S. Blair USN (Ret) made thirteen patrols on five different submarines during the Cold War and his naval career spanned three decades. He served aboard the USS *Tunny* (SSG-282) over four years, and served on several other submarines besides the *Tunny*, including:

(1) USS *Blackfin* (SS-322) for three years. During this time, his ship participated in "Operation Iceberg," the first underwater exploration of the Arctic ice pack performed by submarines. He served on the *Blackfin* in 1948, when she made the second of thousands of intelligence-gathering patrols made against the Soviet Union by U.S. submarines during the Cold War.

(2) USS *Tiru* (SS-416) for three and a half years. *Tiru* was the first high speed submerged "Guppy" snorkel submarine in the Pacific fleet, and the first diesel-powered submarine to snorkel submerged (thirteen days) from Hawaii to San Diego, California. They surfaced off San Diego the morning the North Koreans invaded South Korea. He subsequently made five war patrols in *Tiru* during the Korean War while operating out of Japan, in support of the United Nations forces in Korea. During one patrol, he was depth charged by an enemy country

he will not name, and was trapped in an enemy minefield for four hours before the ship made its way to safety. The ship "snagged" two mine cables, but managed to slip out of the trap.

(3) USS *Robert E. Lee* (SSBN-601) for two years, placing her in commission as Executive Officer of the Gold Crew. He made two deterrent missile patrols in her, operating out of the Holy Loch, Scotland. It was also the first nuclear submarine built in the South.

(4) USS *Daniel Webster* (SSBN-626) for over three years, placing the ship in commission as its first commanding officer. *Webster* deployed on patrol with the Navy's first load of Polaris A-3 missiles on board. He made four deterrent missile patrols, operating three out of Rota, Spain, and one out of the Holy Loch, Scotland.

(5) USS *Queenfish* (SSN-651) was the first nuclear attack submarine. One of his duties was to inspect the nuclear power plants and engineering personal on nuclear attack submarines in the Pacific.

After he retired, Blair served as a Nuclear Technical Specialist and Division Manager with the Omaha Public Power District in Omaha, Nebraska. During this time, he assisted in completing and bringing Fort Omaha, then in New York, for Gibbs & Hill, Inc., a large international power engineering company headquartered in New York City. In 1984, he retired from that company as a Vice President in New York. In retirement, Blair continued to work as a nuclear power consultant for three more years. He and his wife, Baylor, lived in Hot Springs Village, Arkansas, for eighteen years before moving to Omaha, Nebraska, in July 2001.

Captain Blair was a member of the Diamond Chapter WWII Submarine Veterans of Arkansas.

[The information regarding the submarines Captain Marvin S. Blair, USN (Ret.), served on was gathered from his career article requested by U.S. Submarine Veterans of WWII Associate Commander, Jim Stephens, and printed in the Arkansas Diamond Chapter newsletter, October 2006.]

* * *

Charles Davis, who served on the USS *Tunny* (SSG-282) from 1960 to 1962, and Tom Krohn ETCS (SS) (SSN-682) 1978–1979, USS *Tunny* (SSN-682), are members of the USSVI Twin Lakes Base, Mountain Home, Arkansas.

USS *Tunny* (SSG-282), Charles Davis

"Recalling Brutal Winter Days of Old at Electric Boat Shipyard"

Written by John Steward

Reprinted with permission from *The Day*, March 14, 2013

There's nothing colder than the steel hull of a submarine fully exposed to a freezing New England winter.

Building submarines is a tough job under the best of conditions, but frigid weather tests even the hardiest of souls and the materials they work with.

A few decades ago, submarine construction areas at Electric Boat offered workers little protection from the elements. Boats sat high on supports, wide open to punishing wintry winds. The subs' towering hulks cast long, cold shadows through the shipyard. Workers braved the cold rain and snow as best they could in a brutal environment where any continual contact with the cold steel hull froze any part of a person that wasn't already frozen.

A young Sam Grills, hired as a shipfitter, walked down the main yard hill into EB's shipyard for the first time on October 15, 1956. It was a year after the *Nautilus*, the world's first nuclear powered sub, rode the ways into the Thames River and nautical history. As a shipfitter, he would install tanks, decks, and various hull structures.

Every step that day took the Westerly resident deeper into the daunting environment of building submarines.

EB's shipyard of old was a world unto itself. With multiple boats under construction, hundreds of workers labored simultaneously. The yard was alive with dynamic sights and sounds, a robust community orchestrated by the shouts of men with frosty breaths visible in frigid air, the noise of motors, cranes, drills, grinders on steel, and hammers pounding material into submission.

Brilliant welding sparks snapped, crackled, and shot fireworks into the smoky, pungent air. Unrelenting air compressors and other machinery screamed, making conversation difficult. Smoke, dust, and debris turned faces under hard hats black with dirt and grime. Shipfitters, pipefitters, welders, carpenters, mechanics, riggers, painters, electricians, engineers, and other tradesmen swarmed over the vessels.

Trucks, handcarts, and couriers scurried about, delivering supplies over, under, and around hoses and cables, scaffolding, tool bins, stockpiled materials, ladders, and temporary outdoor workbenches.

Imagine this covered in freezing air, wind, rain, or snow and you get the idea. It was a long cold day's work filled, no doubt, with thoughts of hearth and home.

"When I arrived in 1955, there were two Peruvian boats under construction in the North Yard," said Grills. "The North and South yard building ways were covered between the railroad tracks and the road bordering the shipyard and the floors were dirt." The "ways" were tracks that held subs under construction and upon which the finished product would one day glide triumphantly into the Thames River. They were partially covered, but not enough to keep the biting winter winds off the water from finding their way into the very bones of workers.

Grills spent the winter of 1956–1957 laying out hull plates and structures for the USS *Skipjack* and the USS *Triton*. With hulls exposed to the weather, snow would have to be kept clear of the ship, work areas, and anything requiring welding, which is pretty much everything.

Temporary shelters or sheds had to be built and protective coverings erected over work areas to protect against heat loss when preheaters were used to warm the hull prior to welding. Steel has to be a certain temperature before welding to ensure a solid bond and avoid cracking.

Many years later, Grills clearly remembers trying to stay warm: "During the winter, warmth came from salamanders [stoves] filled by the learners and apprentices, whose duty was to keep the stoves supplied with buckets of coke," he said. "The salamanders would glow cherry red when boosted with compressed air hoses and anyone would be roasting on the side facing the stoves and freezing on the side not facing the stoves."

Shipbuilders are a touchy breed and Grills remembers the midday break "where every afternoon there would be an assembly line of boilermakers [a shot and a beer] lined up on the bar across the street ready for the noon lunchtime workers." Anything to ward off the cold.

Much has changed since the 1940s and 1950s. The ways are gone, replaced by new technology, main construction areas are enclosed, and EB has become very good at controlling the environment. Even the lunch break outside the gates is a thing of the past. Rough and tumble has been replaced with professionalism, efficiency, and safety.

There's a strong pride in this business of building the submarines that defend our country. Having survived several cold winters in the shipyard, after fifty-six years Sam Grills is still at it today. He eventually moved into design as company needs changed.

Through the years of World War II alone, the men and women of Electric Boat sacrificed through hot summers and biting cold

USS *Sea Fox* (SS-402)

USS *Sea Fox* (SS-402) was a *Balao*-class submarine. *Sea Fox* was commissioned on June 13, 1944. She earned four battle stars for her World War II service and four campaign stars for service during the Vietnam War.

Information taken from https://en.wikipedia.org/wiki/USS _Sea_Fox_(SS-402)

USS *Sea Fox* (SS-402), a WWII *Balao* boat

CAPTAIN NORMAN "RED" STEIN

"What's a Submarine Commander Doing with the Likes of Doris Day and Mary Martin?"

Written by Colonel Wilcox, who flew a B-17 bomber in Europe in World War II.

First published in *50plus Senior News* and reprinted with permission from *50plus Senior News* and Col. Wilcox, Capt. Stein, and Megan R. Joyce, Editor, *50plus Publications*[9]

Norman "Red" Stein says, "In New Kensington High School, near Pittsburgh, I was a lot more interested in football, basketball, boxing, and girls (not necessarily in that order) than I was in study."

His parents seemed to have noted that, too, and he was soon enrolled as a sophomore at Valley Forge Military Academy. He says, "That absolutely changed my life. It introduced me to a life of discipline and study."

He still played sports, of course, competing in football, boxing, and track. He also participated in three years of Army ROTC. He remembers that in his sophomore year, he won the school's championship, boxing against the captain of the football team, which gained him much respect on campus.

But it was his play as a halfback on the school's first undefeated football team that helped win him a scholarship to North Carolina State University.

---

[9] http://50plUSSeniornewspa.com/news/2014/may/02/whats-submarine-commander-doing-likes-doris-day-an/?page=2

USS *Sea Fox* (SS-402), Norman Stein with Doris Day

There he played one year before deciding to try for a nomination to the U.S. Naval Academy. He was fortunate enough to land that, and he played sports there, winning the boxing crown at 155 pounds as a plebe. He also played jayvee and varsity football before suffering a knee injury that ended his football career.

At the academy, he met Dusty Dornin, a much-medaled hero submariner of World War II, who impressed him by picturing life in submarines as providing the inclusiveness and fraternity of an infantry platoon.

So, when graduating from the academy in 1952, submarine service was much on his mind. However, he was required to first have a year in surface ships. Assigned to an amphibious landing ship, he headed for the Pacific.

He especially remembers their serving as station ship in Hong Kong for twenty days, their role being ready to evacuate U.S. citizens as might be needed.

He also recalls with affection knowing the owner of Hong Kong Old Mary's shop, where seamen from everywhere bought cloth for civilian suits that were tailored for them overnight.

Then he got his wish, for the submarine duty that was to occupy him for nineteen years. Leaving from Key West, he started by patrolling the North Atlantic, where his sub was once hit by the most vicious storm he had ever seen.

They had to surface to recharge the sub's batteries, and he says, "The seas were so high that, on the surface, we couldn't use the air intakes to get air to the engines. We had to use our snorkel, and we were barely able to avoid its being awash. We lost all our communication antennas, all radar, and one periscope. When we submerged, we were still rolling 15° even at a depth of 150 feet."

That Atlantic duty was followed by two years as an instructor at the Submarine School at Groton, Connecticut. Then it was off to the Pacific Northwest, making patrols off Okinawa, Japan, and other islands.

He remembers one time in 1963, when they returned to Long Beach and were picked to be the sub to appear in a Doris Day movie, *Move Over, Darling*, where Doris played the role of a wife whose passenger plane goes down in the Pacific and who is marooned on a Pacific Island for five years before being picked up by a submarine and returned to the U.S.

And, surprisingly, that was not Stein's only touch with Hollywood. Once, when his sub pulled into Okinawa, Mary Martin was touring with the entire cast of *Hello, Dolly!* It packed a huge field house. Stein and his crew enjoyed the show.

Then he sent Mary a card inviting her and the whole cast to tour his submarine, the *Sea Fox*. She sent a kind note, explaining why the schedule wouldn't permit that, and Stein sent her a certificate making her an Honorary Member of the *Sea Fox* crew. Mary later sent him an autographed playbill cover for the show, writing on it, "Hello, Red, from an Honorary Crew Member of the *Sea Fox*, Mary Martin."

Years later, when Mary was starring on Broadway with Robert Preston in *I Do! I Do!* Stein sent her a note saying, "The commanding officer of a submarine has the right to visit honorary members of his crew at any time."

Mary's husband then called Stein to say that tickets for him and his wife Lonnie would be waiting for them at the box office. They, of course, attended. And after the show, he and Lonnie were ushered backstage to visit with Mary.

Stein says, "You can't believe how warm and cordial she was to us."

Stein spent his last Navy years at the Pentagon, where he was responsible for the administration of the Submarine Intelligence Program. He remembers once going to the White House to conduct a briefing for a Strategy Committee.

How did that go?

"Well," he says, "I got to make Henry Kissinger laugh, so I guess it went okay."

Stein retired from the Navy as a captain in 1978 and spent twelve years working in his dad's insurance business and "playing a lot of golf." He and Lonnie then moved close to Annapolis and built a home there.

In 2007, another Navy captain friend invited him and Lonnie to look at a retirement community in Lancaster. They came, found it suited them perfectly, and they've lived there with their Husky, Balti, ever since. They love it and wish only that they had found Lancaster sooner.

Written by Norman "Red" Stein

Reprinted from the *Sea Fox* Association's newsletter "Below the Deck" / Winter 2014, permission given by editor, Joel Greenberg

When Joel Greenberg invited me to write an article for the *Sea Fox* publication, he mentioned I was one of the two remaining commanding officers of the 402 still alive. At the age of eighty-five, with classmates and friends passing away on a weekly/monthly basis, Joel's comment added to my reflective mood. How did I get to become CO of *Sea Fox*, and who and what were the major influences in my life? So, if you will permit me license, I'll ramble on and share my reflections with you.

It all started in the mid-30s, at the usual Saturday afternoon movie, admission ten cents. The featured film was *Shipmates Forever* with Ruby Keeler, on location at the Naval Academy. After seeing this movie, I was determined to enter the academy. However, as I was progressing through junior high, focusing on football, basketball, baseball, and girls (not necessarily in that order), my parents decided that a change was required if my goal was to be achieved. So in the middle of my sophomore year, January 1944, I was off to Valley Forge Military Academy in Wayne, Pennsylvania.

Valley Forge changed my life. The discipline, military atmosphere, and athletic opportunities were exactly what I needed. When I graduated from VF in '47, I spent a year at North Carolina State and completed my fourth year of Infantry ROTC. I had visions of a career in the Marines, but in those days, only former Marines or those with a family relationship of Marines could enter the CORPS upon graduation. It was at that time in 1950 that I came under the influence of Captain "Dusty" Dornin, Class of 1935, who was on duty at the Naval Academy, and who convinced

USS *Sea Fox* (SS-402). Photo inset shows the U.S. Coast Guard *Sea Fox* (WPB 87374), named after the USS *Sea Fox* (SS-402). Photo contributed by George Arnold, USS *Sea Fox* 402 Association.

me that the atmosphere aboard a submarine and between officers and crew resembled that of a lieutenant and his infantry platoon. Ironically, "Dusty" was a one-time skipper of *Sea Fox* and one totally dedicated to his crew.

I relieved Bob Vaughn in Pearl Harbor on June 25, 1965, and left for WestPac the following morning. My bride still accuses me of giving her a peck on the cheek as I boarded the boat, fulfilling a dream. I inherited a boat with a well-trained and professional wardroom and crew, with two consecutive "E's" earned in '63–'64. The professionalism and training were soon demonstrated as we approached Tokyo Bay in a dense fog. All special sea detail stations were manned promptly and the plotting began. Soon a contact was reported in a crossing pattern, traveling north. We slowed. As the situation became classic, I reflexively ordered "all stop." Backed full and dead in the water, we watched a barely visible coastal freighter cross our bow. The event foretold of a successful deployment.

We successfully completed an SAR mission in Tonkin Gulf. With 150 feet of water, it was not the most comfortable location. Dozens of junks kept us company during the pitch-black nights.

We also had the good fortune to see Mary Martin perform in *Hello, Dolly!* while in port in Okinawa for a weekend liberty. As a result, my wife and I had a chance to visit with "Honorary Crew Member" Martin on Broadway several years later. We earned an "E" for the year and soon entered overhaul at Hunter's Point Shipyard in San Francisco. Post overhaul, we again deployed. The highlight of this effort was a collection effort in the South China Sea.

I was relieved in Yokosuka and soon found myself at the Pentagon, responsible for the administration of the Submarine Intelligence Program and getting missions' approval by the chain of command. My experience aboard *Sea Fox* could not have been better. The Chief's Quarters, Wardroom, and Crew were superb at that time. If I had the opportunity to choose any boat to command, I could not have chosen a better one than *Sea Fox*.

From the Pentagon, it was a year at the Army War College, CO SubDiv31, EA & Aide to ASN I & L and finally, CO *Sacramento* (AOE-I), before retiring in 1978. I have been most fortunate in knowing and working for many illustrative submariners: Gene Fluckey, Dusty Dornin, Mike Rindskopf, Jon Boyes, Dom Paolucci, Fritz Harlfinger, Dennis Wilkenson, Pat Hanmfln, and Maury Horn. My best skipper was Whitey Klinefelter when I was executive officer of *Blackfin*.

My best retirement submarine experience was the *Sea Fox* reunion in 2011, when I met former shipmates John Norman with his wife, Jean, and Leonard Tunnell and his wife, Lynda. Their remarks would have made Dusty Dornin happy.

My warmest regards to all of you *Sea Fox* alumni. Stay healthy. May our traditions continue to inspire others.

Sincerely, Red Stein.

"Those Who Forget History Are Doomed to Repeat It."

Written by Joel M. Greenberg

From the USS *Sea Fox* (SS-402) Association newsletter, "Below Decks Log" / Winter 2014

This saying appears in many different forms, but the earliest version is probably that of the poet and philosopher George Santayana: "Those who cannot remember the past are condemned to repeat it."

Another great philosopher, Yogi Berra, said: "When you come to a fork in the road, take it." A great baseball catcher or not, this is still a very prescient statement. Every decision in life is a fork in the road. (Engineers call this Pert Chart and Decision Tree Analysis.) Even standing still is a fork— staying or moving forward. Why have I brought this up? It is all about the forks in the road that happened to get me (and I suspect all of us) here—the past.

So let me tell you about my past. In 1935, Donald

USS *Sea Fox* (SS-402), Joel M. Greenberg

USS *Sea Fox* (SS-402), Joel Greenberg in the mess

Dericks joined the Navy. He worked his way up the ranks and retired from the Navy as a lieutenant. Following the bombing of Pearl Harbor, his close cousin Lee joined the Navy because Donald was a sailor. Lee spent the war on active duty and four more years in the Naval Reserve. To this day (at age ninety-one), Lee continues to think fondly of the Navy and says he often regrets not staying for a career. This positive Navy view led Lee's son to join the Navy in 1967 at the height of Vietnam conflict. I am Lee's son.

I am also a Diesel Boater. Note that I did not say I *was* a Diesel Boater. That time spent was so significant to my life that I certainly would not be where I am today if it were not for the three boats in which I served. I pushed for diesel submarines because as a kid I read all the books about submarine exploits in WW II. It was the end of the era, and the recruiters and the OCS staff said I could not go to diesel boats. I was persistent, so I got there. They were right. I put two of my three boats out of commission. I am one of the younger ones of that era, still six years away from Holland

186

USS *Sea Fox* (SS-402), Joel M. Greenberg

Club eligibility. I stayed in the Navy and eventually ended up in the Supply Corps. My dolphins opened many a door, and those Keepers of the Doors knew I sailed on diesel boats. My diesel boat experience continues to this day to make life better.

I am where I am today because Donald Dericks made a choice in 1935. We Diesel Boat Submariners have built a history (our past) that provides an important legacy for our current and future (nuke) forces. So remember—Officer, Enlisted, Nuke, Diesel Boater—we are all Brothers of the Phin with a common past built on all the forks in the road taken. That is why the USSVI Creed, "To perpetuate the memory . . ." is so important. It is so we do not forget our past. It is who we are today, and it is important to our future.

[A portion of this story appeared in the column "Minivan Mama: Who Is Donald Dericks" by Stefanie Campos (Joel Greenberg's daughter) and Joel M. Greenberg. Stephanie was the former copy editor for the *Imperial Valley Press* and a graduate of San Diego State University's journalism program.]

* * *

Credit goes to my *Sea Fox* skipper, Walt Stammer, for supporting me as *Sea Fox* supply officer, and helping me be selected as a supply corps officer and be integrated into the Regular Navy. I went from *Sea Fox*, when we decommissioned, to weapons officer on the *Catfish*. When *Catfish* was decommissioned, I went to Supply Corps School, then joined the *Hammond*, which we affectionately called the *Franny Maru*, on the Vietnam gun-line. This was my longest Navy sea tour, two and a half years.

After serving in three twenty-six-year-old submarines, it was nice joining a brand new ship. I relieved the commissioning supply officer out there a week after my skipper, Pete Doerr, relieved the commissioning CO. And, for my time on board, I was the only supply corps officer in ComCruDesPac to be certified as a

USS *Sea Fox* (SS-402), Joel M. Greenberg

CDO (command duty officer), because I wore line-officer dolphins. Someplace in my collection there is a letter to that effect. When I was on board long enough to become the senior department head, I was also appointed as senior watch officer. Thank you, Walt Stammer and my fellow "Brothers of the Phin."

— Your Editor, Joel.

JERRY FOSS

Written by Jerry Foss

I served on USS *Sea Fox* (SS-402) from January 1969 to November 1970. The *Sea Fox* had recently returned from a six-month tour with the 7th Fleet, and from then until 1969, she continued to rotate between training operations out of San Diego and duty with the 7th Fleet in the western Pacific.

189

We were asked to photograph an old sub being sunk, *Redfin* (SS-272) or *Redfish* (SS-395), as I recall. *Catfish* was the boat shooting the torpedo. As I understand it, boats that had an excellent war record were sunk rather than mothballed [saved].

Anyway, we were at periscope depth—fifty-eight to sixty feet—and ready to shoot photos. A skeleton crew got the *Redfin* under way at slow speed and then was evacuated by helicopter. Once the fish (torpedo) was in the water, somehow it headed for us rather than the boat it was to sink. I had heard about "flooding negative," but this is the only time I experienced it. I was in the conn, as I was a quartermaster, or at least was studying to be one. Just like in the movies, we heard the torpedo overhead as we descended rather rapidly. By the time we leveled off we were at about test depth, 400 feet or so.

The next exercise training came when we were operating out of Subic Bay in the summer of 1970. We were running war games with New Zealand or the Australian Air Force; can't remember. We were running dark and hiding, and they were looking for us. Cloud cover was 100 percent, maybe at 1,500 feet. It was night out and we had surfaced recently. I was on the bridge. One of their planes had been up high and cut its engine to glide down so as not to be heard by us. About the time it came out of the clouds, it turned on a huge light that seemed to illuminate our entire world. It immediately restarted its engines. We definitely were outsmarted and "caught."

The last incident I recall in my two years of service was around an individual. I was hot bunking (two or more crew members in one bunk). The new "nonquals" often get issued a blanket and a pillow while sharing a bunk in the after battery with someone while that person is on watch.

Each submarine has holding tanks to hold the sewage inside the boat, and every so often it has to be pumped out. Pressurizing the tanks requires nobody flush a head (toilet) during that process. Everyone on the boat must learn how to run every system in case of emergency. Once they accomplish this task, they are awarded "dolphins." Anyway, another crew member after battery woke up to relieve himself. He was almost sleepwalking as he entered the head and leaned forward. When he accidently opened the flush valve, the tank below was pressurized for pumping, and the opening he created caused a vent and some of the contents of the tank bolted and splashed all over his face. There was quite a noise as the pressurized air escaped, but it was then almost immediately followed by another loud noise as the guy emptied his stomach onto the floor. It is crazy what one recalls and what stays quiet and hidden inside of our daily life in submarines.

* * *

Jerry Foss QM3 (SS) served from January 1969 to November 1970. Foss is a member of the USS *Sea Fox* Association. After returning to civilian life, he worked in his brother's car stereo business from 1974 until 1984, then took a couple of years off. He began his current career in 1988, where he is now in real estate sales and consulting at Windermere Professional Partners at University Place, Washington (state).

* * *

In November of 1970, the USS *Sea Fox* (SS-402) was declared unfit for further service. She was decommissioned and her name was struck from the Navy list on December 14, 1970. *Sea Fox* earned four battle stars during World War II and four campaign stars for service during the Vietnam War. Commanding Officer to July 1969 was Harold M. Richardson and from July 1969 to December 1970 it was Water H. Stammer Jr.

Sea Fox participated in World War II, Korea, and Vietnam. It conducted many dangerous Cold War exploits as mentioned in *Blind Man's Bluff: The Untold Story of American Submarine Espionage*, by Sherry Sontag and Christopher Drew, with contributions by Annette Lawrence Drew.

DICK MURPHY IC3-SS

"I Remember"

A submarine poem story by Dick Murphy
December 14, 2009

Here's to us, one and all,
Who heard the message and answered the call
To break away from the old mainstream
And live our lives on a submarine.
Sub School gave us the chance to pass the test,
To declare that we were The Best of the Best.
When we left New London with orders in hand,
We all headed out on different courses for distant, faraway lands.
Some went east coast, some went west,
But no matter where you ended up, your first boat's the best.
You reported on board not knowing what to think,
But now you're known to all as a nub and a dink.
You learn about Tradition and learn about Pride,
You learn about Honor and the men who have died.
You learn about the heritage that's been passed on to you
Because now you're considered one of the crew.
You study that boat from bow to stern,
From the conning tower to the bilges—
It's your duty to learn
Where and what makes that boat go,
How it operates and in what direction it flows,
How to charge those batteries and keep them alive,
Or how to rig the boat for dive.
Draw those systems fore and aft,
Blow the shitters, check the draft.

These are duties that you must glean
When you live your life on a submarine.
When you've learned all there is to know about your boat,
You show 'em you know it, by your walk-through vote.
You go before the Qual Board, card in hand,
Where they question and grill you to beat the band.
And when you think you can take no more,
They tell you to wait just outside the door.
For what seems like eons, time stands still,
And when they call you in, you feel quite ill!
But they congratulate you for doing so good
And welcome you into their Brotherhood.
Right of passage declares that you must drink your "fish,"
And the tacking on process is not something you wish.
But you wear those dolphins on your chest with pride,
Because down deep in your heart, you know you're Qualified.
It seems like yesterday, it seems like a dream
That I truly lived on a submarine.
Most Boats are gone, a memory of time.
I wonder what happened to that crew of mine?
The Old Boats that are left are all museums,
And even if you rode 'em,
You have to pay admission to see 'em.
So here's to us, those that remember,
Who rode the boats out in all kinds of weather.
To those past, present, and even the future,
To those young, hardy lads who still love adventure.
So let's lift our glasses and have a toast
To the memory of those daring young sailors and their undersea
boats.

* * *

"Any man or woman who may be asked in this century what they did to make life worthwhile in their lifetime, I think can respond with a great deal of pride and satisfaction, 'I served a career in the United States Navy.'"

— President John F. Kennedy, August 1963

* * *

CURTIS GRANT
"Submarine Career as a Spook Rider"
Written by Curtis Grant,
CTICS (SS) USN (Ret)

Submarine Spook Rider Curtis Grant. Photo courtesy of Mary Nida Smith.

I served aboard several submarines for a short time, adding up to a total of thirteen months. My time was spent arriving aboard, performing my duties, and getting off.

I was a CTI (Cryptologic Technician Interpretive branch) and spent most of my Navy time at shore bases. I entered the Navy as an electronic technician recruit. After boot camp at San Diego, I went to Imperial Beach to learn how to operate a teletypewriter and took a test to see if I had potential to learn a foreign

Submarine Spook Rider Naval Communication Base Alaska sign

language. I scored high enough to go to the Naval Intelligence School in Washington, DC, where I studied Russian. This was in 1958, Cold War time.

My first assignment was at the Naval Radio Facility, Sidi Yahia, Morocco, where I worked in the Processing and Reporting Office. In the summer of 1959, the P&R office was instrumental in identifying and (with the help of Naval Air P3 aircraft) locating one of the first Soviet merchant vessels carrying missiles to Cuba.

After an advanced Russian language course back at the NIS (Navy Investigative Service), I was assigned to TUSLOG Det 12 in Istanbul, Turkey. During three years at this base, we monitored a couple of surface-to-surface missile shots in the Black Sea and kept tabs on any Soviet units leaving the Black Sea via the Straits of the Bosporus.

I was stationed at the Naval Communications Station (NCS/NSGA Naval Security Group), Adak, Alaska, from the spring of 1964 until October 1966. Here, again, I was assigned to the P&R office. This time, however, we were monitoring the Soviet fishing fleet in the Bering Sea. There were a lot of trawlers working that area, and they often encroached into area claimed by Canadian and U.S. treaties.

[Fishing assistance programs gave the Soviets an excuse to include administrators, advisors, technicians, propagandists, and others not directly associated with the assistance project. This often allowed the Soviets to enhance their political presence and expand the bilateral naval relationship. It was certainly the case in Egypt, where the Soviets in 1964 built a port facility for fishing, and eventually naval, vessels. Their presence in Egypt allowed Moscow to expand its naval presence to the Indian Ocean. Today the Soviet navy maintains facilities at Aden and Socotra Island, South Yemen, Ethiopia's Dalek Island, the Seychelles Islands, and it has an extensive naval cooperation relationship with India.]

A few were lost during very severe storms, and one captain of a trawler sustained a serious injury while quite near Adak. The fleet tug attached to Adak Naval Station was sent to assist and brought the captain back to the hospital. My boss, a senior chief who was quite fluent in Russian, interviewed the captain during his stay in the hospital. Regardless of the exchanges made, when the captain was able to return to his ship, the senior chief was not allowed to go along; only the tug's crew was. They had a good time swapping cigarettes and lighters and anything else they could get their hands on for this little trip.

Late in 1966, I accepted orders to Goodfellow Air Force Base, San Angelo, Texas, as an instructor. [As part of Air Education & Training Command, Goodfellow's main mission was cryptologic and intelligence training for the Air Force, Army, Coast Guard, Navy, and Marine Corps.] During this tour, I was advanced to chief petty officer. Here I was, instructing young petty officers on how to do things I had not yet done—mainly what their jobs were to be if they volunteered for submarine duty. I was already a volunteer, but had not been accepted yet.

197

Lo and behold, my next orders were to Naval Security Group, Kami Seya, Japan. I made my first Special Operations, Counter Terrorism Database (SPECOP) run during the summer of 1970 on board the USS *Carbonero* (SS-337), while Captain Joseph J. Dunn, USN 259 (April 1969–December 1, 1970) was aboard. It was my one and only trip on a diesel boat. It was also the longest SPECOP of the six I made during the four years I was in Japan. I was the senior enlisted team member on four of the trips. The teams were comprised of four CT branches—linguists, Morse code operators, special signals technicians, and maintenance personnel. Depending on which boat the team was to go aboard, there would be from eight to twelve, sometimes more, men on the team.

The boats in which I made SPECOPS were the *Carbonero* mentioned above, the USS *Snook* (SSN-592), USS *Gurnard* (SSN-662), USS *Hawkbill* (SSN-666), USS *Guardfish* (SSN-612), USS *Pintado* (SSN-672), and USS *Drum* (SSN-677). Oh, you say, that is seven boats! Right you are! The team boarded the *Hawkbill* for a trip, but this boat was ordered to take on another task and we transferred to the *Guardfish* for the SPECOP.

I qualified on the USS *Pintado* (SSN-672) on my fifth trip. The captain and the rest of the *Pintado* crew pinned my "dolphins" on me at the end of the trip in February 1973. My tour in Japan would soon be over, but I made my last trip on the USS *Drum* before I was next assigned to shore duty at GCHQ [Government Code & Cipher School], Cheltenham, England—a long transfer when such transfers were not being done.

I spent three years at Cheltenham and then returned to the States, to Fort Meade, Maryland, home of the National Security Agency. I became an instructor again to finish my Naval career and then worked at NSA for fourteen years before retiring *again* and moving to Mountain Home, Arkansas.

* * *

Curtis "Curt" Grant CTICS (SS) served from 1957–1981 and retired January 1988 (the All Naval Security Group members—Service Roster) as Senior Chief Cryptologic Technician Interpretive. He is the commander of USSVI Twin Lakes Base, Mountain Home, Arkansas (2007–present).

* * *

The USS *Drum* (SS-228), a *Gato*-class diesel-electric submarine, has been at home in Mobile, Alabama for nearly forty years now. Since opening as a museum on July 4, 1969, the *Drum* has been a silent reminder to thousands of visitors of the 52 submarines and over 3,600 submariners who made the ultimate sacrifice in WWII. Still, many people throughout the southeast United States have no idea such a rare naval WWII icon is right in their own backyard. Now residing on land nearby the USS *Alabama* (BB-60) battleship in Battleship Memorial Park lies the USS *Drum* (SS-228), the oldest American WWII submarine in existence.

USS *Drum* patch

[Post WWII: After the War, the Government Code & Cipher School changed its name officially to GCHQ and moved its headquarters to Eastcote in Middlesex (1946), and later to Cheltenham in Gloucestershire (1950s).]

The following is from the website Spook Group at http:// spookgroup.tripod.com/. This website is a Virtual Reunion. This is for all you Unsung *(apologies to TC)* Heroes of the Cold War, The Sub-Surface Cryptologic Direct Support Element CTs, more commonly known by Fast Attack Submariners as "Spook Riders."

> We ate their food,
> We wasted their water,
> We breathed their air, but...
> *"We Were Not There!"*

USS *Sunfish* (SSN-649)

USS *Sunfish* (SSN-649) was a *Sturgeon*-class attack subma-
rine. She was commissioned on March 15, 1969. In 1996,
Sunfish made history with her 1000th dive, before she was
finally decommissioned that same year.
   *Information taken from https://en.wikipedia.org/wiki/USS
Sunfish(SSN-649)*

MARK R. CLARY

"Christmas I Remember Best: Ocean depths fail to dampen spirit of Christmas"

Written by Mark R. Clary

The Christmas that will remain forever etched in my memory was
devoid of snow and sleigh bells. There were no chestnuts roasting on an open fire and no aroma of spicy apple cider. There was
no turkey, no mistletoe, and no Santa in the department store.
There were no Christmas trees. There were no presents to unwrap.
I witnessed the powerful impact of the spirit of Christmas many
years ago—several hundred feet beneath the surface of the Atlantic Ocean.

USS *Sunfish* (SS-649), Mark R. Clary

Our submarine had just completed a seven-month tour of duty in the Mediterranean at the height of the Cold War. We were scheduled to return to our home port of Charleston, South Carolina, two days before Christmas. The thought of seeing family and friends after such a long absence made our excitement almost impossible to contain, and returning just in time for that wondrous holiday created unbearable feelings of anticipation. Unfortunately, our enthusiasm was short-lived. While passing through the Straits of Gibraltar, we received emergency orders to locate and track a Soviet submarine that had been detected near a strategic port in Spain.

The feeling of discouragement formed a huge black cloud that enveloped each man aboard. We knew full well that our window of opportunity for a return by Christmas was already extremely small, and this detour would mean no hugs from loved ones on Christmas morning. Even though we performed our assigned task in a professional manner, it added five days to our schedule, and the successful completion of the mission did little to relieve the pain of homesickness that seemed to consume everyone.

Shortly after completing that final mission, at a time when things felt especially gloomy, I picked up a colored grease pen used for keeping the maneuvering room status board current, and in the lower right-hand corner I drew a small red and white candy cane. When I had finished, the twinkle in the rest of the eyes of the men in the room was unmistakable, and there was just a hint of a smile in their countenances.

Over the next few days, I began to add bits and pieces of the season to the board. One morning I drew a tiny snowman, the next a Christmas tree with ornaments. The following day found Santa and his sleigh flying above rooftops. During each four-hour shift, I added a little something more—until finally a shining star looked down on a small Nativity scene, and the work was complete.

And that's when it happened. Men who had worked so hard for so long to maintain their rough exterior could be heard singing Christmas carols throughout the submarine. Men who had always taken a special pride in how callous they were began to ask, "Who remembers the second verse to 'Silent Night'?" Men who had refused to acknowledge their spiritual side assisted one another in recalling the words to "Away in a Manager." The atmosphere aboard the submarine had changed completely. The feeling of depression and sadness had been transformed into one of "peace on earth, good will to men."

Then, on Christmas day, the unthinkable happened. The captain, who always stayed at the forward room section of the boat to monitor sonar readings and maintain visual sightings from the periscope, walked aft to the rear of the submarine and entered the Maneuvering Room.

Even though we were surrounded by large pumps, motors, hydraulic systems, turbine generators, and the main propulsion shaft, a deafening silence fell over us. I tried to envision life in the brig—the Navy's term for jail. I thought of how simple grease pencils and a piece of Plexiglas may have just cost me a successful term of naval service, because I knew that using the status board as a makeshift Christmas card was clearly a violation of Nuclear Regulatory Commission procedures.

For several more minutes, not a word was spoken. Then the captain of the nuclear submarine, the commander of one of the world's most powerful strategic military weapons, said in a soft and almost reverent voice, "Merry Christmas, men." He turned and left the room, walked slowly back to the forward part of the boat, and quietly closed the door to his private stateroom.

I learned that day the Spirit of Christmas could be felt by all men, even the most hardened sailors. I learned that the warm light of the season can be felt anywhere, even on board a submarine far beneath a cold and dark sea. I learned that there is a sweet spirit that can be awakened within each of us through the simplest of means—even a small red and white candy cane.

* * *

This story by Mark R. Clary was published Friday, December 19, 2014, as one of seven winners in the *Deseret News* annual "Christmas I Remember Best" writing contest [Salt Lake City, Utah].

Mark Clary EM2 served aboard the USS *Sunfish* SSN-649, and it was during these nine months when the Christmas events occurred. Clary received his training at the Nuclear Power School in Bainbridge, Maryland, and Prototype Certification in Saratoga Springs, New York.

USS *Daniel Webster* (SSBN-626) / USS *James Monroe* (SSN-622)

USS *Daniel Webster* (SSBN-626) was a *Lafayette*-class ballistic missile submarine (FBM). She was commissioned on April 9, 1964.

Information taken from https://en.wikipedia.org/wiki/USS _Daniel_Webster_(SSBN-626)

USS *James Monroe* (SSBN-622) was a *Lafayette*-class ballistic missile submarine. She was commissioned on December 7, 1963. She served with the United States Navy from 1963 to 1990.

Information taken from https://en.wikipedia.org/wiki/USS _James_Monroe_(SSBN-622)

WAYNE "KIRK" SMITH
"Panama Canal Transit"
Written by Wayne "Kirk" Smith

I had the opportunity to do two transits of the Panama Canal on two of the boats that I served on. The first was on March 7, 1970, when I was on the USS *Daniel Webster* (SSBN-626). I remember that specific date because there was a total eclipse of the sun while we were in the canal. The weather was great, and we had a barbeque using fifty-gallon cans that had been cut in half so that we could put charcoal in them to cook the hamburgers.

We were traveling west in Gatun Lake, and the USS *Guardfish* (SSN-612) was traveling east. This was the first time that two nuclear submarines passed each other while in the Panama Canal Zone. After completing the canal transit, we continued on to Pearl Harbor, had a change of crews, and the Blue crew took the boat on to Guam. I made four patrols out of Guam, transferring in March 1972 to Dam Neck, Virginia, for shore duty.

The second time I went through the canal was in August 1989 on board the USS *James Monroe* (SSN-622). Once again, the

USS *Guardfish* (SSN-612) and USS *Daniel Webster* (SSBN-626) in the Panama Canal, photo courtesy of Jeff Kelly

USS *Daniel Webster*
(SSBN-626) shellback

weather was great, and we had another barbeque. A major difference: no total eclipse of the sun. I did have a rather unique thing happen, though. I was the chief of the boat (COB), and as such, I was responsible for making sure that we had plenty of toilet paper on board for the duration of the underway period. The rule of thumb is one roll per man per week. I had transferred to the *Monroe* shortly before we left Charleston, South Carolina, and really did not have a chance to check out all of my lockers prior to getting under way. So, on the way to the canal, I realized that I didn't have enough toilet paper. Well, when a boat goes through the canal, we have an opportunity to get some fresh food, so I told the senior chief storekeeper to order a case of toilet paper, so we were set until we could get to San Diego and I could get plenty more.

We did something unusual after exiting the Panama Canal Zone. Our commanding officer had arranged for us to go south

USS *Daniel Webster*
(SSBN-626) Wayne
"Kirk" Smith

and cross the equator. This is something that the SSBN's don't normally get to do. When a Navy ship crosses the equator, we have a crossing the line ceremony. Those individuals that have previously crossed are known as "shellbacks," and the others are "pollywogs." It is quite involved, and a lot of fun for everyone—rather messy and dirty, but still fun.

USS *Daniel Webster* (SSBN-626) shellback certificate

Also, while we were in warmer waters, we surfaced the boat and allowed the crew to go topside and get some sun. Unfortunately, we didn't have a swim call. This was part of the last underway for the *Monroe*, for we were taking her to Puget Sound Naval Shipyard in Bremerton, Washington, for decommissioning.

USS *Skipjack* (SS-184)

USS *Skipjack* (SS-184) was a *Salmon*-class submarine. She was commissioned on June 30, 1938.

Information taken from https://en.wikipedia.org/wiki/USS _Skipjack_(SS-184)

The Famous "Toilet Paper" Letter

On a submarine, everything you need must be requisitioned. The following story illustrates what can happen when requisitions are not fulfilled in a timely manner. Portions of the memo referenced below were read by Cary Grant's character in a movie called *Operation Petticoat*. The actual memo, the famous "toilet paper" letter, was written in June 1942 by Commander James Wiggins Coe (USS *Skipjack*) to the supply officer at Mare Island Naval Base near San Francisco. It can be found at the USS Bowfin Museum & Park in Honolulu.

Sadly, Commander Coe was in command of the USS *Cisco* when she was lost with all hands in September 1943.

USS *Skipjack* toilet paper memorandum, from the Naval History and Heritage Command archives, Washington, DC

USS *Skipjack*

June 11, 1943

From: The Commanding Officer

To: Supply Officer, Navy Yard, Mare Island, California

Via: Commander Submarines, Southwest Pacific

Subject: Toilet Paper

Reference: (a) (6048) USS HOLLAND (5148) USS *SKIPJACK* Reqs. 70-42 of July 30, 1941.

           (b) SO NYMI cancelled invoice No. 272836

Enclosure: (A) Copy of cancelled Invoice.

           (B) Sample of material requested.

1.   This vessel submitted a requisition for 150 rolls of toilet paper on July 30, 1941, to USS HOLLAND. The material was ordered by HOLLAND from Supply Officer, Navy Yard, Mare Island, for delivery to USS *SKIPJACK*.

2.   The Supply Officer, Navy Yard, Mare Island, on November 26, 1941, cancelled Mare Island Invoice No. 272836 with the stamped notation "cancelled - cannot identify". This cancelled invoice was received by *SKIPJACK* on June 19, 1942.

3.   During the 11-1/2 months elapsing from the time of ordering the toilet paper and the present date the *SKIPJACK* personnel, despite their best efforts to await delivery of subject material have been unable to wait on numerous occasions, and the situation is now quite acute, especially during depth charge attack by the "back-stabbers".

4.   Enclosure (B) is a sample of the desired material provided for the information of the Supply Officer, Navy Yard, Mare Island. The Commanding Officer, USS *SKIPJACK* cannot help but wonder what is being used by Mare Island in place of this unidentifiable material, once well known to this command.

5.   *SKIPJACK* personnel during this period have become accustomed to use of "Ersatz," the vast amount of incoming non-essential paper work, and in so doing felt that the wish of the Bureau of Ships for "reduction of paper work" is being complied with, thus effectually "killing two birds with one stone".

6.   It is believed by this Command that the stamped notation "cannot identify" was possibly an error, and this is simply a case of shortage of strategic war

material, the *SKIPJACK* probably being low on the priority list.

7.   In order to cooperate in our war effort at small local sacrifice, the *SKIPJACK* desires no further action to be taken until the end of the current war which has created a situation aptly described as "War is Hell."

—J.W. Coe

* * *

Here is the rest of the story:

The letter was given to the yeoman, telling him to type it up. Once typed and upon reflection, the yeoman went looking for help in the form of the XO. The XO shared it with the OD and they proceeded to the CO's cabin and asked if he really wanted it sent. His reply, "I wrote it, didn't I?"

As a side note, twelve days later, on June 22, 1942, J. W. Coe was awarded the Navy Cross for his actions on the S-39.

The "toilet paper" letter did, indeed, reach Mare Island Supply Depot. A member of that office remembers that all officers in the Supply Department "had to stand at attention for three days because of that letter." By then, the letter had been copied and was spreading throughout the fleet and even to the president's son, who was aboard the USS *Wasp*.

As the boat came in from her next patrol, Jim and crew saw toilet-paper streamers blowing from the lights along the pier and pyramids of toilet paper stacked seven feet high on the dock. Two men were carrying a long dowel with toilet paper rolls on it with yards of paper streaming behind them as a band played coming up after the roll holders. Band members wore toilet paper neckties in place of their Navy neckerchiefs. The wind-section had toilet paper pushed up inside their instruments and when they blew, white streamers unfurled from trumpets and horns.

As was the custom for returning boats to be greeted at the pier with cases of fresh fruit/veggies and ice cream, the *Skipjack* was first greeted thereafter with her own distinctive tribute—cartons and cartons of toilet paper.

This letter became famous in submarine history books and found its way to the movie *Operation Petticoat*, a copy eventually coming to rest at the Navy Supply School at Pensacola, Florida. There, it still hangs on the wall under a banner that reads, "Don't let this happen to you!" Even John Roosevelt insured his father got a copy of the letter.

USS *Raton* (SS/SSR/AGSS-270)

USS *Raton* (SS/SSR/AGSS-270) was a *Gato*-class submarine. She was commissioned July 13, 1943, and received six
battle stars for her World War II service.

*Information taken from https://en.wikipedia.org/wiki/USS
Raton(SS-270)*

JOE SABOL GM1 (RET) (SS-270)
1943–1945

JOHN "BIFF" BAKER ENC/SS (AGSS)
1960–1967

First, a glimpse into a few of *Raton*'s war patrols for World War
II:

Starting on August 4, 1944, on her fourth war patrol while at
120 feet, seven-eighths more than a total of fifteen minutes, we
took on depth charges of a total of forty-one. The boarding party
and deck recovery team were awarded the Bronze Star.

The fifth war patrol was for fifty-five days, from July 18 to
September 19, 1944. Explosions from aerial bombs . . . close . . .
escort now closing in . . . went deep . . . many depth charges . . .
four came close so they moved from the area near the shore.

USS *Raton* (SS/SSR/AGSS-270), photo from
http://ss270.com

Duration of her sixth patrol was fifty-seven days. Weather
conditions decreased rapidly, near typhoon proportions at times.
October 1944, fired six torpedoes, no hits . . . enemy escort closing in . . . went deep. Received fifteen depth charges fairly close.
Sabol was in the forward torpedo room at the time, saw a bright
red light flare type light, could have sworn the torpedo loading
hatch opened and closed. The induction value gasket blew, flooding the hull induction lines.

During December 1–4, 1944, the *Raton* underwent voyage
repairs. The USS *Raton* (SS-270) was awarded six Battle Stars for
service in World War II.

* * *

Joe Sabol was a member of the USS *Raton* (SS-270) decommissioning crew on July 1943. Sabol was the historian for the U.S.

USS *Raton* (SS/SSR/AGSS-270) crew members

Submarine Veterans of WWII for many years of dedicated service. Without Joe's help and encouragement, the reunions, crew listing development/maintenance, and the USS *Raton* webpage at http://ss270.com/ would not have been. Joe Sabol's story, "Submarine Joe" was published in *Ordinary Heroes*, a book written by Sarah J. Nachin.

John "Biff" Baker (Chief Engineman) served on the USS *Raton* (SS/SSR/AGSS-270), known as the "Raiding Rat" for seven years (1960–1967). "The best years of my life. There is no boat like your qualifying boat. The officers and crew were known throughout the submarine force as the 'Funny Farm' because we had a crew who were good at their jobs, but had fun both aboard and ashore. I'll miss her till I draw my last breath." Biff Baker is a lifetime member of the USSVI Submarine Base, Mountain Home, Arkansas, and is still a member of the San Diego Base he helped start in the early seventies. He served with Jerry Jacks, a longtime friend.

The Life of a Submarine Man

Poet unknown

My home is the hull of a "pig,"
Those death-dealing wolves of the deep,
A buck for a bed where you sleep foot-to-head,
While the air blowers lull you to sleep.

The chow is OK, and so is the pay
And we sail in fair weather or foul.
We know one and all that the crew's on the ball,
So long as they put up a growl.

For days at a run we don't see the sun,
And our nerves become taut with the strain.
In the darkness we stealthily rise from the sea,
And ere dawn we take cover again.

We wait for one thing—to hear a shrill ring,
And the skipper's voice dead calm and steady,
"Enemy off port bow! Man torpedo tubes now!"
And the answer comes, "Torpedoes ready!"

"Fire one!" calls the old man. His voice is still cool.
The ship holds its breath, then a shudder.

The Life of a Submarine Man

"One hit!" calls the skipper; the men grimly smile,
"Fire two—three! There, that got her!"

For them it's all over. For us, just begun.
The real game of nerves lies in wait.
For now we're the hunted, the depth bombs come close,
In God is our trust and our fate.

We've taken her down to the bowels of the sea,
And sit as one man with no sound.
We listen and count 'em and pray,
as the ash cans explode all around.

That last one was close! Now they start to recede.
We continue to hide in our lair,
Till when hours have passed we proceed with all speed,
And once more God has answered our prayer.

Back to home port we go; our job is well done,
And we swagger as only men can,
And through hell and high water continue to live,
The life of a Submarine Man.

Author unknown, reprinted from Volume One of the *U.S. Submarine Veterans of World War II—A Military Publication* by Fine Books Division of Taylor Publishing Company. Copyright 1986, by the Submarine Veterans of World War II Association and Taylor Publishing Company.

The Submarine Veterans of World War II

The organization called the Submarine Veterans of World War II was formed on September 30, 1956. Enlisted men and officers who were attached to a submarine or a submarine relief crew between December 7, 1941, and September 2, 1945, are eligible for membership.

The Federal Charter was certified by the 97th Congress of the United States of America, Public Law 97-83 on November 29, 1981, by President Ronald Reagan, and presented to Andrew M. Gasper, National President of the United States Submarine Veterans of World War II.

The back cover of their quarterly magazine *Polaris* read: "The purpose of this organization is 'to perpetuate the memory of those shipmates who gave their lives in submarine warfare; to further promote and keep alive the spirit and unity that existed among United States Navy Submarine crewmen during World War II; to promote sociability, general welfare and good fellowship among its members; and [to] pledge loyalty and patriotism to the United States Government.'"

The magazine *Polaris* was the longest running magazine dedicated to submariners of World War II. The magazine was named after the North Star, the guiding point for the ancient mariners. For many years, artist Stephen Petreshock painted the covers.

The publication started out as a four-page pamphlet with Andy Stark as editor until 1959, when Bill Taylor became the new editor. The name change was submitted as "Polaris" by the ladies' auxiliary president, Gloria Unrein. In August 1960, the first issue was released. Editors included Frank Hamilton (1961), George Hamilton (1963), Ed Bland (1965), George Hamilton (again, 1967), Paul Stolpman (1968), Erst Rosing (1969), Don Levange (1970), Harry Fisher (1972), Hugh Lowder (1980), and Bill Wolfe (1985). Until his death in 2014, Bill Wolfe continued his dedication, bringing news from all the chapters to submarine veterans.

As of 2006, Submarine Veterans of World War II organizations continued in 33 states. Finding volunteers became more difficult as health problems arose and death took its toll. Today many organizational bases have been decommissioned. As of 2008, the veterans of World War II were dying at a rate of 1,000 a day, including members of the "Silent Service." Many were only seventeen years old at the time of their service. Today, they are mostly in their eighties and nineties. According to the National WWII Museum in New Orleans, as of 2014 they are dying at a rate of 555 a day. These dedicated men, in part, provided the freedoms we enjoy today.

Today, as health problems have plagued our veterans—first slowly, then quickly—the silent service members are on their last patrol. A younger group is forming. They mingle among the old sailors, listening to their sea stories and hoping to keep their legacy alive by passing their stories down to another generation.

WWII Submarine Patches & Battle Flags

The men created World War II Battle Flags to keep an unofficial record for each submarine of enemy ships they sank while on war patrol. The rising sun version of the Japanese flag represents

Dick Jarenski and Sue Rainey of the USS *Sterlet* (SS-392) Association honor the submarines of World War II with a display of boat patches at the Veterans Memorial Museum in Branson, Missouri.

a warship sunk, and the "meatball" represents a merchant vessel sunk. The submarine logo patch is also featured in the middle of the flag.

The "Silent Service" used the patch on their foul-weather jackets and their boat's flag that wasn't displayed until reaching port. While out to sea, the members of the crew designed and sewed most of the flags and patches for their boats.

For more information, read *War Under the Pacific (World War II)*, by Keith Wheeler and the editors of Time-Life Books, 1980.

USS *Nautilus* (SS-168)

USS *Perch* (SS-176)

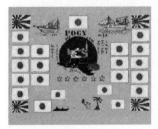

USS *Pogy* (SS-266)

USS *Puffer* (SS-268)

USS *Puffer* (SS-268)

USS *Billfish* (SS-286)

USS *Bowfin* (SS-287)

USS *Archerfish* (SS-311)

USS *Blenny* (SS-324)

USS *Quillback* (SS-424)

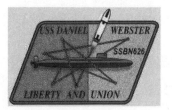

USS *Daniel Webster* (SSBN-626)

USS *Nautilus* (SSN-571)

USS *Skipjack* (SS-184)

Typical U.S. Submarine Cutaway
Showing Compartmentation

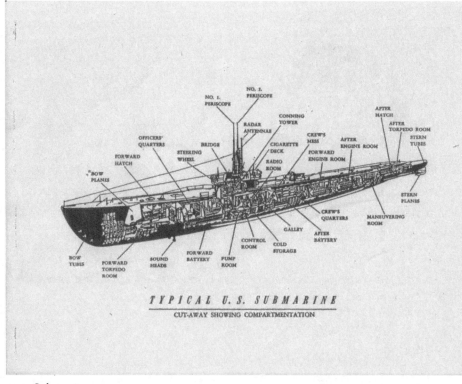

Submarine cutaway

Retirees—When Can I Wear My Uniform?

Retirees may wear the uniform corresponding to the rank or rating indicated on the retired list. The grooming standards presently in effect for active duty personal apply, and the uniform must conform to Uniform of the Day or the uniform occasion.

Occasions for Which Wearing a Uniform May Be Appropriate:

- Memorial Services
- Military Weddings
- Military Funerals
- Military Balls
- Patriotic parades on national holidays or military parades or ceremonies in which any active or reserve military unit is participating.

At meetings or functions of associations formed for military purposes, uniform may be worn to and from the event, but travel must be completed on the day of the event.

The uniform may be worn when instructing a cadet corps or similar organization at an approved institution.

Retirees are eligible (if recalled) for a uniform clothing allowance, if member has been inactive for more than three months and has not received a uniform allowance within four years before recall. Allowances will be based on existing prices at time of recall.

WHEN UNIFORM IS NOT AUTHORIZED

Wearing of the uniform is prohibited in connection with personal enterprises or activities of a business nature. Also, when participating in any demonstration, assembly, or activity whose purpose is furtherance of personal or partisan views on political, social, economic, or religious issues. Exception is when authorized for bonafide service or observance.

Uniform is not required on AMC flights.

MILITARY TITLE USAGE

Military retirees are allowed to use their military title subject to certain restrictions and good judgment. The use should not discredit the Navy or Department of Defense. Such use in connection with commercial enterprises is prohibited—with or without intent to give rise of any appearance of sponsorship or endorsement by the Navy or Department of Defense.

MEDALS AND AWARDS

Information and guidance on personal decorations, campaign and service medals, and other awards are contained in SECNAVINST 1650.1.

For proper wearing of medals and badges, Navy Uniform Regulations (NAVPERS 15665) "Request for Verification and Issuance of Medals on Unit Awards" should be addressed to: National Personnel Records Center, 9700 Page Blvd., St. Louis, MO 63132 (if retired for more than six months). If retired less than six months, contact: Naval Reserve Personnel Center (Code 41), 4400 Dauphine Street, New Orleans, LA 70149-7800.

Glossary

After WRT tank - or water round torpedo tanks, are variable ballast tanks located in the forward and after torpedo rooms, for flooding or draining the torpedo tubes.

Ballast - weight to maintain proper stability.

Banca - small native outrigger.

Bilge - lower part of the vessel where waste water and seepage collects.

Blue water - deep water.

Bow buoyancy tank - extra tank to provide more buoyancy forward when surfacing or in an emergency situation.

Bow planes - horizontal rudders at the submarine's bow, help to give initial diving angle and to coordinate the plane's stem to control depth.

"Close aboard to the stern" - a Navy phraseology meaning short distance to the rear of the boat.

COMSUBPAC - Commander Submarine Force USN Pacific Fleet.

Escorts - ships or aircraft used to protect a merchant ship or convoy.

Fish torpedo - self-propelled torpedo.

Forward trim - variable ballast tank used to adjust the submarine's weight and tilting movements.

Grapnel - a piece of equipment that looks like a huge saltwater fishing line with several gigantic hooks to clamp around an object to pull it upward.

Head - toilet.

1FF (Identification Friend or Foe) - a radar signal that identifies planes, ships, boats, etc., as friend or foe and is only transmitted by aircraft. Aircraft are the ones who use it.

JP, Sonar Sound - a manual train. It is turned by hand. JP is the Navy term for sonic listening gear. The J means that it can be used for listening only. The second letter P indicates the model.

Knots - each knot is a nautical mile per hour. A ship's speed is measured in knots, or one nautical mile per hour.

Lanyard - rope attached to pull the hatch down.

Lifeguard duty - when the boat has orders to go to sea to rescue downed airmen.

List - a leaning to one side, as of a ship.

Mustered - gathered.

New construction - the building of a boat. The sailor has to help as he learns the ins and outs of how a submarine worked/ticked.

Ping - sonar makes a ping when passive.

Plane sonar - a term first used in World War II to describe a system, Sound Navigation and Ranging, based on the reflection of sound waves in the air. (Sonar is used below water.)

Plank owner - an individual who was a member of the crew of a ship when that ship was placed in commission.

Port - nautical term indicating the left side.

Radar - based on the reflection of radio waves in the air. It is used above water.

Refits - repairs and service such as taking on fuel.

Regain lost trim - level the boat to retain a zero bubble.

Screws - the ships' propellers.

Scuttle - the act of deliberately sinking a vessel.

SD radar - The earliest radar installed in the fleet boat, operated from the conning tower and only vaguely directional. It was capable of warning that a plane was within about six miles of the boat, but couldn't really pinpoint a bearing, or give much in the way of information.

Shears - the structure on the submarine that supports the periscopes and radar antenna.

Silent running - when the boat is below water, everything is shut down (off), so the enemy cannot pick up sounds on their sound gear to locate and destroy a boat by dropping depth charges.

SJ radar - surface search radar, shows range and bearing contact.

Smoking lamp - When the smoking lamp was out, it meant no smoking cigarettes on the submarine, and when it was lit, it meant you could smoke.

Sonar - a term first used in World War II to describe a system, Sound Navigation and Ranging, based on the reflection of sound waves underwater using mainly active sonar, which sent out audible pings. (Plane sonar is based on information that comes from sonar used in the air.)

Sonarman - one who operates the sonar device.

Sound - used to detect enemy vessels by the sounds of their engines and for the water depth. Sound stimulates the sense of hearing whenever vibrations take place, and the soundmen can tell from these what and who is approaching the submarine.

Soundman - a crew member on sound in the conning tower who used his ears to hear up to fourteen miles away. Some claimed they could tell the different sounds in the water up to fifty miles away. They had to tell the difference between sea creatures, enemy, or friendly boats. The captain and the crew's lives depend on the soundman.

SP - air research.

Stern planes - the pair of horizontal rudders at the submarine's stern, used to control the angle of the boat.

TAD - temporary additional duty.

Tin can - torpedo.

Tubes - torpedoes.

Wolf pack - three or more submarines that went on war patrols together.

Zero bubble - indicates level; level the boat to retain a zero bubble.

For more definitions and phraseology go to:
http://www.maritime.org/fleetsub/chap2.html
http://www.valoratsea.com/glossary.html

Bibliography

50plus Senior News, On-Line Publishers, Inc., Editor Megan R. Joyce. http://50plUSSeniornewspa.com

The All CT Service Roster. http://www.navycthistory.com/all_members_service_roster_intro.html

All Hands, Magazine of the U.S. Navy. http://www.navy.mil/ah_online/department_arch.html

America's Navy, Commander, Submarine Force, Atlantic. http://www.navy.mil/local/sublant/

American Submariner magazine (USSVI), Editor Charles "Chuck" Emmett. Arkansas Inland Maritime Museum. http://aimmuseum.org/the-american-submariner/

C-SPAN's *American History TV,* American Veterans Center Conference, Wounded Warrior Project, Kia Hunter [permission from C-SPAN] (including USS *Nautilus* (SS-168) CPO Hank Kudzik—The Battle of Midway) October 27, 2012. http://www.c-span.org/video/?309083-5/battle-midway

"The DBF [Diesel Boats Forever] Pin." http://www.submarinesailor.com/history/dbfpin/dbfpin.asp

Dictionary of Naval Fighting Ships. http://www.ibiblio.org/hyperwar/USN/ships/danfs/SS/

Fleet Submarine website. www.fleetsubmarine.com

The Fleet Type Submarine Online: "Submarine Air Systems." From a series of submarine training manuals that was completed just after WW II, describing the peak of WW II US submarine technology. http://maritime.org/doc/fleetsub/air/index.htm

The Goat Locker. www.goatlocker.org

Historic Naval Ships Association, War Patrol Records, Jeff Nilsson. http://www.hnsa.org/doc/subreports.html

"History of the National Publication," by Bill Wolfe, editor of *Polaris*. www.subvetpaul.com/SagasIndex.html

Hullnumber.com. Website created for the purpose of providing a means for shipmates to keep in touch with one another. www .hullnumber.com

Introduction to the stories of the fifty-two boats lost during WWII, by Paul Witmer. http://www.subvetpaul.com/ LostBoats/52BoatsIntro.htm

Library of Congress Veterans History Project. http://loc.gov/vets/ vets-portal.html

Military Acronyms and Abbreviations. http://militaryacronyms.net

Military Terms and Definitions. http://www.militaryterms.net/

Movie poster *Hellcats of the Navy*, and book cover, *Hellcats* based on "Operation Barney." Pacific War book review. www.subsowespac .org/books/hellcats.shtml

National Archives: Military Records. http://www.archives.gov/ research/military/index.html

Naval Historical Foundation. www.navyhistory.org

Naval History & Heritage Command. http://www.history.navy.mil/

Naval History and Heritage Command: Dictionary of American Naval Fighting Ships [DANFS]. http://www.history.navy.mil// research/histories/ship-histories/danfs.html

NavSource Naval History: Photographic History of the U.S. Navy—Michael Mohl, Battleship & Submarine Archive Manager (Photos). http://www.navsource.org

Navy Spook Submarine Riders get together to swap UNCLAS stories and life experiences. http://spookgroup.tripod.com/

Of Ships & Surgeons: Notes on Maritime Medicine—Past and Present. http://ofshipssurgeons.wordpress.com

PigBoats.com. http://pigboats.com Ric Hedman TN (SS), USS *Flasher* (SSN-613) (Plankowner), USS *Cusk* (SS-348) TAD Rider, Webmaster.

Polaris. Official magazine of U.S. Submarine Veterans WWII.

Ron Martini's Submarine World Network. "The world's largest submarine directory listing 1000+ links to submarines of ALL nations and ALL periods of history. A major communication network for USSVI and USSVWWII." http://www.submarinemuseums.org/links.html

Russell, Dale. *Hell Above: Deep Water Below.* (1995) http://www.amazon.com/Hell-Above-Deep-Water-Below/dp/096438499X

Smith, Steven Trent. *The Rescue: 40 Americans Trapped in the Philippines During World War II, a Set of Secret Japanese Battle Plans, and the Submarine that Saved Them.* (2001) http://www.amazon.com/The-Rescue-Steven-Trent-Smith/dp/B002L4QO6W

St. Marys Submarine Museum in Georgia. [Facebook] https://www.facebook.com/pages/St-Marys-Submarine-Museum/121502876248?sk=timeline

Submarine Museums. http://submarinemuseums.org

SubmarineSailor.com. "Where submariners stay in touch." http://www.submarinesailor.com

The Day Publishing Company, established in 1881 by John A. Tibbits, publisher of *The Day*, a daily newspaper covering a 20-town region in eastern Connecticut with a daily and Sunday readership of nearly 100,000, and http://www.theday.com, a website generating more than 4 million page views a month.

U.S. Naval Operations in the Korean War. http://www.nj.gov/military/korea/factsheets/navy.html

U.S. Navy Commander, Submarine Force Atlantic, COMSUB-PAC, Official government site. www.public.navy.mil/subfor/hq

U.S. Navy website. www.navy.mil

U.S. Submarine Veterans of WWII, Diamond Chapter newsletter (Arkansas).

U.S. Submarine Veterans of World War II: A History of the Veterans of the United States Naval Submarine Fleet. 1986, 1988, 1990. Fine Books Division of Taylor Publishing Company. http://www.amazon.com/United-States-Submarine-Veterans-World/dp/B000FT96UG

Undersea Warfare, magazine of the U.S. Navy. http://www.public.navy.mil/subfor/underseawarfaremagazine/Pages/default.aspx

Undersea Warfare, magazine of the U.S. Navy. [Facebook] https://www.facebook.com/USWMagazine

United States Submarine Veterans, Inc. (USSVI). Submarine veterans after World War II who are honoring all men and women who have served on submarines in all wars and conflicts. A list of submarine memorials and artifacts listed by boat is a USSVI Internet Project. www.ussvi.org

United States Submarine Veterans, Inc. (USSVI)—Charleston Base

United States Submarine Veterans, Inc. (USSVI)—Dallas Base—Commander Leonard Tunnell

United States Submarine Veterans, Inc. (USSVI)—Tucson Base—Commander Joel Greenberg

United States Submarine Veterans, Inc. (USSVI)—Twin Lakes Base—Curtis Grant

USS *James Monroe* Association (SSBN-622). http://www.USSjamesmonroeassn.org/

USS *Nautilus* Alumni Association (NAAI). http://www.USSNautilus.US?crewmembers.htl

USS *Puffer* (SS-268) (SSN-652). www.USSpuffer.org

USS *Raton* (SS-270). http://ss270.com

USS *Razorback* (SS-394), Arkansas Inland Maritime Museum.
http://aimmuseum.org/USS-razorback/

USS *Sea Fox* (SS-402) website. George Arnold, Webmaster http://
seafoxss402.homestead.com//

USS Submarine POWS of WWII. http://www.subvetpaul.com/
POWs.htm

USS *Tinosa* (SS-283). www.HullNumber.com

Water Encyclopedia: Science & Issues. Submarines and submersibles. http://www.waterencyclopedia.com/St-Ts/Submarines-and
-Submersibles.html#ixzz3Z8LwhxmC

Wheeler, Keith. *War Under the Pacific: World War II.* Editors of
Time-Life Books (Hardcover). http://www.amazon.com/
War-under-Pacific-World-II/dp/080943377X/ref=la_B001H
6TW46_1_2?s=books&ie=UTF8&qid=1404575179&sr=1-2

The Worldwide CT Community and Our Naval Security Group.
http://www.navycthistory.com/

About the Author

Mary Nida Smith has written for newspapers and magazines in Oregon, Washington, Idaho, Missouri, and Arkansas. She is a former board member of The Friends of the Library (Donald W. Reynolds), historian and columnist for Ozark Regional Arts Council, founder of Twin Lakes Writers and Creative Writers & Illustrators, and is a member and former vice president of Ozarks Writers League.

Smith has written for military magazines and authors four blogs. She is former newsletter editor for the Arkansas Submarine Veterans of World War II, a lifetime member of Wives of Submarine Veterans Inc., and is a former member of Military Writers of America.

Submarine Stories of World War II, First Edition (published by Red Engine Press, 2008) was available in three military museums.